"When Freud's ideas were first introduced, they seemed obscure arcane, and they never became reader—or patient—friendly. In *Wisdom from the Couch*, Jennifer Kunst builds a much-needed bridge by enabling the sophisticated field of psychoanalytic theory and practice to make common sense without compromising its complexity. One of the many virtues of Dr. Kunst's presentation is the way in which she uses the work of Melanie Klein and makes it accessible to a wide audience. Her chapter on 'proper dependence,' 'ripening to obedience,' and 'inspired independence' (Chapter Ten) alone is worth the price of this book. She has written a superb work, one that is as masterful as it is timely. She artfully presents a number of theoretical ideas, some complex and others simpler, all with such seamless clarity that the work speaks meaningfully to seasoned psychoanalysts, beginning mental health workers, high school and college students, parents, and others."

—*James S. Grotstein, MD, Professor of Psychiatry, UCLA School of Medicine, Training and Supervising Analyst at the Los Angeles Psychoanalytic Institute and the Psychoanalytic Center of California; Author of* . . . BUT AT THE SAME TIME AND ON ANOTHER LEVEL . . . : PSYCHOANALYTIC THEORY AND TECHNIQUE IN THE KLEINIAN/BIONIAN MODE

"Dr. Kunst has written a remarkably readable book about what is often a difficult quest for the meaningful life. Her ability to take the complex psychoanalytic theories of Melanie Klein and synthesize them with her spiritual beliefs in a way that is easy to follow is a refreshing and welcome addition to the integration of psychology and spirituality. Despite all our complicated theories and scientific efforts to identify the secrets of a life well lived, I agree with her that it all essentially comes down to one thing: love. Those who read this book will be more equipped to be better lovers of others, themselves, and God."

—Mark W. Baker, PhD, Executive Director of La Vie Counseling Centers; Author of JESUS, THE GREATEST THERAPIST WHO EVER LIVED

"In this marvelous book, Jennifer Kunst gives us a highly readable primer on the fascinating therapeutic approach of Melanie Klein, making her case with references to the likes of Shaq O'Neal, *The Velveteen Rabbit*, and St. Benedict. But even more, her 'wisdom from the couch' is offered in terms of a candid and inspiring account of her own spiritual journey."

—Richard J. Mouw, PhD, President Emeritus and Professor of Faith and Public Life, Fuller Theological Seminary; Author of UNCOMMON DECENCY: CHRISTIAN CIVILITY IN AN UNCIVIL WORLD

"One of the most urgent needs for psychoanalysts, for psychotherapists, indeed for the wider world, is to reach down into the depths to discover what is sanity and to differentiate it from madness. Jennifer Kunst clearly knows this, and in this work is doing two jobs: She (1) dismisses defining madness according to a surface symptomology, and (2) opens a gateway to a new way of thinking about this urgent problem. All those who have been scratching their heads and wondering how to find their way to a more sane and meaningful life will—if they are open to Jennifer's guidance—begin to find an answer. This book beckons us to open its pages and read with care and attention."

—Neville Symington, Training and Supervising Analyst, Australian Psychoanalytical Society; Author of THE PSYCHOLOGY OF THE PERSON and BECOMING A PERSON THROUGH PSYCHOANALYSIS

Wisdom

FROM THE

COUCH

Wisdom
FROM THE
COUCH

Jennifer L. Kunst

KNOWING AND GROWING YOURSELF
FROM THE INSIDE OUT

CENTRAL RECOVERY PRESS

Las Vegas

Central Recovery Press (CRP) is committed to publishing exceptional materials addressing addiction treatment, recovery, and behavioral healthcare topics, including original and quality books, audio/visual communications, and web-based new media. Through a diverse selection of titles, we seek to contribute a broad range of unique resources for professionals, recovering individuals and their families, and the general public.

For more information, visit www.centralrecoverypress.com.

Publisher: Central Recovery Press
          3321 N. Buffalo Drive
          Las Vegas, NV 89129

19 18 17 16 15 14   1 2 3 4 5

ISBN: 978-1-937612-61-0 (paper)
      978-1-937612-62-7 (e-book)

Author photo by Diedre Engle. Used with permission.

Quotations from Bhante Gunaratana, *Mindfulness in Plain English* (Somerville, MA: Wisdom Publications, 2011), reprinted with permission from the publisher, www.wisdompubs.org.

Quotations from Bronnie Ware, *The Top Five Regrets of the Dying* (Carlsbad, CA: Hay House, Inc., 2011), reprinted with permission from the publisher, www.hayhouse.com.

Quotations from Ruth Harms Calkin, *Tell Me Again, Lord, I Forget* (Carol Stream, IL: Tyndale House, 1986), reprinted with permission.

Quotations from *Letters to a Young Poet* by Rainier Maria Rilke, translated by M.D. Herter Norton. Copyright 1934, 1954 by W. W. Norton & Company, Inc., renewed © 1962, 1982 by M. D. Herter Norton. Used by permission of W. W. Norton & Company, Inc.

Publisher's Note: This book contains general information about psychoanalytic theory and practice, as well as personal growth and development. Central Recovery Press makes no representations or warranties in relation to the information herein; it is not an alternative to medical advice from your doctor or other professional healthcare provider.

Our books represent the experiences and opinions of their authors only. Every effort has been made to ensure that events, institutions, and statistics presented in our books as facts are accurate and up-to-date. To protect their privacy, some of the names of people, places, and institutions have been changed.

Cover design and interior design and layout by Marisa Jackson.

In memory of my mother, from whom all blessings flow.
In Helen Keller's words, "All the best of me belongs to her.
There is not a talent or an aspiration or a joy in me
that has not been awakened by her loving touch."

TABLE OF
CONTENTS

FOREWORD

IN THIS IMPRESSIVE BOOK FOR the general reader, Jennifer Kunst finds wisdom not only from her training and practice as a psychoanalyst, but also from her experience of everyday life, from films and children's books, and from her religious training and experience.

Dr. Kunst spreads her net widely, but her aim is traditional. She sets great store by truth, and by growth and development, and her heart is set on finding peace. As she expresses it, "Peace in the world, peace with your enemies, peace in your families, and peace within yourself. Peace is perhaps the most valuable thing in all of life."

Having this goal does not mean that Dr. Kunst ignores the problems that arise along the way, nor does she ignore the horror and violence that we see around us when we read the news or watch TV accounts of wars, terrorist attacks, and counterattacks.

She searches for "a bigger life and a bigger God out there." In the past she has worked with criminally insane patients and has encountered "people from other races and cultures, poverty, violence, addiction, crime, severe mental illness, and a host of other contexts so far from my own." All this has broadened and deepened her understanding, so that she is far from an armchair theoretician.

Perhaps most important is her awareness that any belief system can be turned into a fundamentalist creed, whether religious, political, philosophical, or psychoanalytic. In this respect she recognizes how difficult it is to live in the real world with its pain, disappointment, and imperfection, and how tempting it is to turn to a belief in our own omnipotence—a concept that Melanie Klein found to be so central to the human condition. Dr. Kunst suggests that omnipotence commonly involves three related beliefs: a belief in magic, a belief that we can be perfect, and a belief that we will live forever.

It is Jennifer Kunst's experience as a young psychoanalyst that allows her to deepen her understanding of the human predicament. Not content with the isolation of the clinical situation, she applies the knowledge acquired there to the tasks of everyday life. In doing so, she allows readers to reflect on the psychoanalytic dynamics that might be at play in their own lives.

This sensitive and passionate book will interest a wide range of readers, and particularly those who wish to look beneath the surface of beliefs, dogmas, and ideologies. It is so easy to look for magical solutions from an omnipotent deity or an omnipotent ideological system, and in this way to partake of the omnipotence. If we take this route, we come to believe that only our thinking is right and we react with prejudice to other beliefs.

Perhaps the most potent counter to prejudice is knowledge, and Jennifer Kunst has made a valiant attempt to integrate various sources of knowledge and bring them to bear on the contemporary problems of everyday living.

—*John Steiner, MD, Training and Supervising Analyst at the British Psychoanalytic Institute; Author,* PSYCHIC RETREATS *and* SEEING AND BEING SEEN: EMERGING FROM A PSYCHIC RETREAT

ACKNOWLEDGMENTS

AS LONG AS I CAN remember, I have wanted to be a writer. As evidence, there is a photo of me at around age four, sitting at the dining room table on a makeshift high chair of phone books, hunched over an old Royal typewriter, looking like a cub reporter trying to make a deadline. This book, then, is the ripening of that early aspiration and the joyful satisfaction of it.

My mother tended my childhood aspirations with a loving touch, although, sadly, she didn't live long enough to see my dream come true. I am fortunate to still have a father and a sister who remember that photo as if it were taken yesterday, who have always cheered me on as they watched me grow. So, to the family of my childhood, I offer my first thanks.

A book that speaks about the wisdom of psychoanalysis cannot be conceived in a vacuum; to have any real depth, it requires lived experience that can only be found in an intentional community of learning. My community is the Psychoanalytic Center of California (PCC) in Los Angeles. At PCC, adoptive parents, grandparents, aunts and uncles, siblings, and children have taught me, influenced me, fed me, challenged me, and helped me find my voice. In particular, Dr. Mark Hassan and Dr. Chris

Minnick brought to life the concepts of Melanie Klein, both for me and within me. I am forever in their debt and promise to pay it forward.

I am grateful to my group of dedicated patients who have opened their hearts, minds, and lives to me, day after day, week after week, and often year after year. They have given me the gift of meaningful work, and I have learned so much from them. I also extend my thanks to the students who have ventured into my seminars over the past twenty years at Fuller Graduate School of Psychology and Patton State Hospital. The "Church Ladies," too, were enthusiastic learners and the best posse a gal could ever have. Through their hunger for understanding, these patients and students have inspired me to find commonsense ways of describing complex ideas and creative ways to reach them, not just intellectually but at the core.

This book got its real shot with a traditional publisher because of my online platform, *A Headshrinker's Guide to the Galaxy*, so I must thank the editors at *Psychology Today* for giving me the opportunity to write a blog for their website. I extend my thanks to my agent, Linda Roghaar, who through serendipity happened to be going through her inbox when my email query letter came through. The folks at Central Recovery Press, especially Dan Mager, had the life experience in both publishing and mental health that made our partnership such a natural fit. It has been an unexpected blessing that my publishing team could understand my work so deeply, even from the inside out.

A friend once said that your bridesmaids change through the seasons of your life. Those who stand up for you at your wedding may be different from those who stand by you through the birth of a baby, or an illness, or an important milestone such as this. So I thank the bridesmaids who stood by me through the making of this book—Usha Daniel, Gayle Marks, and Helen Nedelman. They loved me, supported me, and jumped up and down with delight at all the right places. I wish Carla Schuler had lived long enough to see this day, but I like to think she is somewhere beaming with pride while hosting a heavenly book-launching party for me with yummy canapés.

Saving the best for last, I thank my husband, Scott Miller. I love that he calls this "our" book because, in so many ways, it is. He has been my unofficial agent, editor, manager, and muse, pushing me to stay in the game and keep setbacks in perspective while bragging about me behind my back. He read every page of this manuscript, taking his time, soaking it in, wrestling and questioning and critiquing in his signature way. I smile when I imagine myself opening the book for the first time and finding a little square of paper that says, "Inspected by STM."

My cup runneth over.

INTRODUCTION

MANY YEARS AGO, I CAME across a greeting card entitled "Ten Things to Make Besides Money." Here is the list: Make merry. Make do. Make sense. Make amends. Make peace. Make waves. Make room. Make time. Make love. Make believe. I loved the innocent wisdom of that list so much, I held onto the card and pinned it to the bulletin board over my desk at work. All these years later, I would be hard-pressed to come up with a better list of things that make for a meaningful life.

To launch our endeavor, let's start with one of the most compelling aspirations on the list: make peace. If you're anything like me, you long for peace. Peace in the world, peace with your enemies, peace in your families, and peace within yourself. Peace is perhaps the most valuable thing in all of life, for, as I shall define it, peace is the basis of so much of what makes for a good and satisfying life, whether it be in high-level matters such as a moral worldview and a sound economy, or in the immediate longings of ordinary, daily life such as a happy love relationship, contentment with one's work, physical health, self-respect, and even a good night's sleep. While it is among the most precious qualities of life, peace—for a whole set of reasons—is one of the most difficult things to make and even harder to sustain.

In one way, "making peace" describes the process of working hard to reconcile our competing needs and desires. We all know about this kind of struggle. We read about it in the news; we struggle with it in the personal politics of the workplace; we watch it unfold at the dinner table and at family gatherings. We humans are just so darn competitive. We claw for power and resist compromise. We love to win and we hate to lose. If peace is about giving up something we value or feel we deserve, we want none of it. This is true whether we are speaking of the external world, like the Middle East, Wall Street, or Main Street, or—as I shall try to show in this book—when it comes to the internal world, the world of the heart and mind.

Peacemaking involves shifting from a competitive mode of relating to one of give-and-take. It is a process that involves finding that delicate balance between fighting for our needs and wants and making concessions out of fairness and respect for another. This is the vital process that we must all undertake to live in greater harmony with ourselves and with one another. Many books have been written about this kind of peacemaking, both from the perspective of our global community and for those engaged in the spiritual, psychological journey toward inner peace. We strive to balance competing motivations: love for self versus concern for the other; the comfort of sameness versus the appeal of risk and growth; the allure of success and power versus the satisfactions of camaraderie and peace of mind.

But the phrase *making peace* has a double meaning. It also speaks to the deeper work involving the relationship between ourselves and reality. This may sound like a funny way of describing it, but I think our relationship with reality is one of the hardest things to face in psychological life. It takes maturity to sort through the realities of complex ordinary life—the highs and lows, triumphs and disappointments, and everything in between—and conclude, "I've made peace with it." In this way, making peace with one's life has a direct link to something else on the list from that greeting card— we are trying to "make do" with a reality that is less than our ideal. We are lending strength to a state of mind that allows us to move forward and get on with our lives.

This approach is at odds with the stuff of the modern self-help movement in which we are encouraged to view ourselves as unlimited potential. This trend is seductive and powerful, offered in both subtle and overt ways in religion, modern psychology, and the New Age movements. We long to believe that we are limited only by the limitations we impose upon ourselves. We are offended at the mere suggestion that we live within boundaries that we cannot change. It is not the American way.

And yet, there are many lessons to be learned throughout the wisdom literature of the great problems that come when human aspirations are not kept in check with human limitations. One thinks of Icarus flying too close to the sun, Sisyphus trying to cheat death, Adam and Eve wishing to know as much as God, or the Israelites building a tower at Babel to reach the heavens. Envy, greed, and grandiosity get the best of us. The global economic turbulence of the last decade heralds this message. Should we listen, we will be reminded at every turn that we are mere mortals, subject to limitations. And one of the great lessons of life is that denying this truth leads to all sorts of trouble and accepting it shall set us free.

As a psychoanalyst, I see my patients struggling every day with this central task—to embrace and work with the life they have been given. I think that we human beings have a deep, natural resistance to this psychological task and that this resistance is a fundamental obstacle in our efforts to change and grow ourselves. It is extremely difficult to look at one's life and say, "This is what I have to work with. This is my personality. This is my raw material. This is the life I've been given—the intellect, the body, the particular sensitivities, the strengths and weaknesses, the parents, the siblings, the children, the culture, the upbringing. This is my history—what I have been given and what I have done with it. I can wish for a different life, but I cannot have it. I must work with what I have." As the saying goes, "We must bloom where we are planted."

This second meaning of *making peace* is foundational to having success with the first. It means that we honor differences, work within the confines of the reality of our situation, and rely on the resources we have rather than nursing grievances or fantasizing about some ideal conditions that will never be. While this approach to life is enormously practical, it is also quite profound. In fact, these truths are at the heart of many spiritual philosophies—from both the East and the West. In particular, I like the Rule of St. Benedict, the guidebook of monastic life that emphasizes stability as the basis for continual conversion. Benedict emphasizes that it is only through commitment to one's life *as it is* that we can grow and develop along the spiritual path. So, too, the Buddhists say that acceptance of the imperfections and impermanence of life is the starting point on the path to self-development and enlightenment—a journey that may take many lifetimes.

Throughout my professional life, I have been engaged in a personal journey of trying to make peace in and with myself. This has not always been easy, for I came to my work as a psychoanalyst along an unusual path. I grew up in a family that had deep religious roots in the mainline Protestant Christian church. For many years, Christian faith has been a guiding star for me, leading me with an ever-deepening desire to be a more thoughtful, balanced, and loving person. It has inspired me to follow a professional path of helping other people, with the twists and turns in the road leading me to training first as a clinical psychologist and then as a psychoanalyst. The religious roots of my path to psychoanalysis are unusual because many psychoanalysts are atheists and most hold the view that religion is something of a crutch for people who cannot face reality squarely.

I was fortunate, however, to grow up among what I call "thinking Christians." Questions, doubts, searching, and deliberation were an essential part of the culture of my religious upbringing. I am grateful for it because I know that this is not the case for many people who are raised in traditional religious families. Even when my path took me in a more evangelical direction at Wheaton College and Fuller Theological Seminary, I was able to become connected with bright people of deep faith who practiced what David Dark calls "the sacredness of questioning everything."[1] This depiction may be surprising, as conservative Christian schools such as Wheaton and Fuller have the reputation of being narrow- and closed-minded. Sometimes that reputation is deserved, although it is not always the case. While faculty and students choose to be guided by a code of faith and conduct, there is still room to question, to search, and, above all, to think.

As I look back on my experiences, those settings were something like a modern monastery for me. Within the self-imposed boundaries of those commitments, there was a home base from which to explore.

Many a classroom discussion or late-night coffee session found us challenging our faith at the frontiers. I have tried to keep that spirit alive as an adjunct professor at Fuller Seminary and in all my work in the years that have followed my work there.

With that said, I also must admit that I have experienced many frustrations with my Christian faith. It has not always been a source of peace, and has even been a source of disappointment, grief, and agitation. I continue to wrestle with its many imperfections and contradictions—both in its theology and in the ways in which the faith is practiced in organized, institutional religion. I have had to wrestle with the commonly held Christian beliefs that the Bible contains everything essential for life and the idea that Jesus is the only way to salvation. I think these are awfully narrow ways of viewing God and leave so much out of the equation. I believe there is a bigger life and a bigger God out there, and I have tried to have the wherewithal to look outside of my religious culture to see what other people are doing in their search for a meaningful life, even in their search for God. Along the way, I have had to make peace with the limitations of my personal faith, as well as the faith of my upbringing and my culture, seeking to cherish and build on the enduring truths while at the same time forgiving the limitations and failures.

I am grateful for the ways in which my work as a clinical psychologist and psychoanalyst has broadened my thinking, largely through in-depth exposure to people with a wide range of life experiences. For the first ten years of my career I worked at Patton State Hospital, where I conducted and supervised therapy with criminally insane patients—mentally ill men and women who had committed violent crimes such as rape and murder. During those days, I tried to walk a mile in the shoes of people whose paths were sometimes beyond my imagination—people from other races and cultures, poverty, violence, addiction, crime, severe mental illness, and a host of other contexts so far from my own.

Both then and now, as a psychoanalyst in private practice, I have intentionally put myself in situations that will burst my bubble. In particular, I often engage in conversations that challenge me to empathically understand people who operate with an entirely different value system from my own—people who have a different attitude toward honesty, fidelity, work, achievement, relationships, family, and the like. I have worked hard to become the kind of therapist who can set being judgmental aside (as much as one can) and be guided by real and genuine curiosity. How did this person get here? How does this way of thinking, believing, or behaving hold together in his or her mind? How does it work for him? What does it cost her? It is a privilege to be granted access to the life of another. I am given the unique opportunity to see another person's life from the inside—an experience that grows me, widens my understanding of the human condition, and helps me question my own assumptions and commitments.

I love my work immensely, but if you think being a psychoanalyst is a picnic compared to being a Christian, think again! Training in a psychoanalytic institute has been likened to being a member of a religious institution[2]—where it is Freud rather than Moses who brought the tablets down from the mountain. No deeply held belief system is immune from being turned into or misused as a fundamentalist creed. As a result, I have discovered that I must make peace with my psychological and psychoanalytic theories too—biased as they are, like religion, by the lens of the pioneers who themselves had limitations, blind spots, and agendas.

But I shall be ever grateful for Sigmund Freud, Melanie Klein, and those who developed their ideas about the life of the mind, the profound influence of unconscious forces, and the techniques that can bring about real, substantial transformation in the lives of those who seek it.

Taking it one step further, I have had to make peace with the limitations of the actual practice of psychotherapy and psychoanalysis—to face the reality that there is only so much that can be done to bring about change within myself and within my patients. I have had to face the disillusionment of my youthful fantasies that we are all created equal and are capable of becoming anything we wish to be. Experience shows that, together with the possibilities of real change, there are also real limitations. I present this sobering reality to my patients and students by suggesting that the kind of change one can expect in a successful, long-term analysis is like changing the course of a ship about ten degrees. While it is a modest, not radical, shift, it will take you in a completely different direction.

———

I think of myself as something of a hybrid in my professional peacemaking journey, trying to blend two systems of thought into a whole where the marriage of Christian faith and psychoanalysis works for me. However, as in any marriage, there are times when it is uncomfortable and challenging. I know that for some people, this mix is like oil and water. Like many of you, I mingle at the dinner party where these topics come up and, soon enough, the arguing and bad feelings begin. There is a way in which I wish to dodge the conversation, but it is something that I care about deeply and so I must push through my own resistances to grow, make a change, and find a new way.

By laying this foundation, I hope to offer a context for the ideas that are to come. Make no mistake—this is not a book about the integration of religion and psychoanalysis. It is a book about the basic principles of psychoanalysis that can be applied to anyone interested in living a more peaceful, fulfilling life. Since I come to psychoanalysis along the path of Christian spiritual practice, my approach may resonate in a particularly harmonious way with those from a similar background. But this is a book for any seeker, religious or not, who is willing to reflect upon his or her life with seriousness and to dig deeper into truths that transcend religion and, in some ways, even transcend psychoanalysis. I believe that the deepest truths have no culture, no religion, and no creed. Deep truths speak to all people and can be applied to all people—and these are the truths that I am going to share in a simple, accessible way.

In order to get to these deeper truths, I will have to strip them of their packaging. I will reduce them to their simplest components. I will try to avoid jargon. I hope to leave the ivory tower. I will have to stray from orthodoxy. I will have to question assumptions. I will play with ideas rather than rigidly uphold them. In an effort to reconcile and make something new, I must challenge what has been long established and perhaps even taken for granted. Unintentionally, I will offend. I will step on people's toes. I will touch and examine a few sacred cows. It can't be helped.

Some people relish that kind of revolutionary attitude, but that is not really my style. And so, I will make every attempt to share my ideas with humility and respect. My motives are to learn, to grow, and to share some lessons I have learned along the way. I want to be of help to the ordinary men and women engaged in the work of developing their own minds in a thoughtful, honest way. I wish to pass on wisdom I have learned from psychoanalysis filtered through my life experiences, and take a next step.

I must make one final note before setting out on this journey. In my effort to pass along the wisdom of psychoanalysis in an accessible way, I will keep theoretical terms and references to a minimum. But, in so doing, I run the risk of giving the impression that I discovered these ideas. I did not discover them. I am a messenger, a translator, and, hopefully, a diplomat. The psychoanalytic theories that I am drawing from have their roots in Sigmund Freud, as all psychoanalytic theories do. I am carrying forward a particular branch of the psychoanalytic tree, which is the work of Melanie Klein and of those who later went on to elaborate on her work.

Melanie Klein was a younger contemporary of Sigmund Freud who considered herself a developer of his ideas, particularly in their application to children. However, she was a pioneer in her own right and extended his theories in an insightful, sometimes radical way.[3] She made waves. She practiced the sacred art of questioning everything, and developed a psychoanalytic model that I think is enormously useful, both in the practice of psychoanalysis and in everyday life. The thrust of her model of the mind is aptly described by the themes of making sense, making do, making amends, making love, and making room for one's whole self. Few people will ever have the chance to be exposed to her wisdom—as the reach of psychoanalysis is so limited, mostly due to the immense investment of time and resources that is needed to learn about it, either as an analyst or as a patient. It is my hope that this book will bring her ideas to a much wider audience, for they are indeed ideas that can lead to that precious state she called "internal harmony," and I call "making peace."

CHAPTER ONE

WHAT YOU SEE IS *NOT* WHAT YOU GET

On the Unconscious Life of the Mind

YOU'VE PROBABLY HEARD IT SAID that insanity is doing the same thing over and over again and expecting a different result. By that definition, we are all sometimes, if not often, insane. Otherwise, how could it be that perfectly intelligent people do such obviously counterproductive things? Why would we do the things we know we shouldn't do, and why would we not do the things we know we should do? Or, to paraphrase social psychologist Jonathan Haidt, why are we so stupid?

The fact of the matter is that we are not really insane. And we're not really stupid. We are human. And human thinking isn't always logical. Our minds are not programmed computers running robotic lives, making decisions in a mathematical way. No, we have human minds that are much more complex than that. Such complexity makes us capable of tremendous creativity and productivity, but it also makes us capable of some serious distortion. We do not see things simply as they are. Our perceptions are altered by our personal psychology—by our emotions, our expectations, our needs, and our desires. As the French philosopher Henri Bergson put it, "The eye sees only what the mind is prepared to comprehend." Our personal filters factor in: Who we are changes what we see.

This is why so much of ordinary life is a mystery to us. This is why, despite our best efforts, we often grow up to repeat the mistakes of our parents. Why a second marriage often winds up just like the first. Why New Year's resolutions rarely lead to meaningful change. Why diets usually don't work and sometimes even make us fatter. In short, this is why we tend to make the same mistakes over and over again, never seeming to learn.

> *So much of what motivates us and concerns us, holds us back, and pushes us forward lies beneath the surface of consciousness.*

There are many ways to explain this phenomenon, but I wish to put forth the psychoanalytic explanation that the unconscious mind is at the heart of the matter. What lies beneath the surface tells the tale.

To use Sigmund Freud's metaphor, the mind is like a glacier. So much of what motivates us and concerns us, holds us back, and pushes us forward lies beneath the surface of consciousness. In everyday life, we do our best to work with what we consciously know—the tip of the iceberg. But because we work at such a surface level, we don't take into account the powerful forces that lie beneath.

There is a story told in the Bible about Jesus giving some advice to his disciples. A couple of his guys were out fishing. They were professional fishermen, so they knew what they were doing. They had spent the whole night casting their nets into the sea. They used all of their usually effective techniques, calling upon all the tricks of their trade. But even with their best efforts, on this particular night they didn't catch a thing. Just as they were ready to throw in the towel and head home, Jesus came along and said to Peter, the lead fisherman, "Push out into the deep water and cast your nets there" (Luke 5:4). I'm sure Peter thought to himself, "Yeah, right. I'm going to take fishing advice from a carpenter's son!" But, reluctantly—and perhaps with a bit of faith—he cast his nets into the deep water. And it turns out that's where all the fish were.

I tell you this story because it shows how essential it is to do two things if you want to get out of your insanity and find your way into a different reality. First, you have to change your technique. And second, you have to go deep.

One of the limitations of contemporary psychology is that so many of the approaches tend to be too shallow. Many types of psychotherapy—helpful as they are—address only the surface of psychological life. Successful treatment outcomes are defined by a reduction in symptoms. Insurance companies want to see quick results, and we do, too. We are seduced by the allure of seven-steps-to-happiness and feel-better-in-ten-sessions-or-less.

But such techniques do not lead to real, lasting change.

Years ago when Shaquille O'Neal was at the height of his basketball career as the center for the Los Angeles Lakers, he spent a great deal of time at the free throw line because he was intentionally fouled so much. Free throws were his weakness, and the other teams knew it. It was a bit painful to watch this enormous and enormously talented athlete shoot the ball so flat from the free throw line, missing shot after shot after shot. I'll never forget when local legend and sportscaster Chick Hearn analyzed the situation. He said that Shaq could not be faulted for failing to practice; in fact, he practiced his foul shot for hours, each and every day. Chick Hearn commented that the problem was that he kept practicing the same shot. No matter how much you practice, he said, you can't change if you have a flawed technique.

Just like Shaq, we need a fundamental and deep transformation. Doing the same thing over and over again won't lead to a different outcome. A surface adjustment isn't going to cut it. If we want to make deep changes, we have to go deep to make them. We have to get to the root of the problem, the heart of the insanity. We have to go below the tip of the iceberg. We need an approach that appreciates the powerful influence of the unconscious. The good news is that if we change at this deep level, the surface changes will follow.

Much of what I want to show you in these pages requires an open mind. The unconscious is difficult to grasp, both as a concept and in its real influence in our lives. It can't be measured in a direct way. It isn't particularly well suited for study in a laboratory. It is known only through inference. It is grasped only by deduction. It is like gravity. You can't see it or touch it, but you know it is real because its effects are real.

So I say to you, the reader, what I say to my students and patients: I can't prove anything about the unconscious to you. I can only show you what I see; it is up to you to decide if it makes sense and if it could be useful to you.

Understanding how the unconscious mind works requires careful study. We must look for patterns, trends, and repetitions so we can get the big picture. But the devil is also in the details, as they say—in the slip of the tongue, in the unintended revelation, and in the dream that haunts us at night. Understanding the unconscious mind requires imagination, intuition, and investigation. It is both science and art. We hear the unconscious not only in the words, but also in the music. We pay attention to what is there, but we also notice what is missing. We must play with ideas rather than be bound by them. We really have to think. We have to be open to the truth conveyed in the saying that there comes a time when the mind takes a higher plane of knowledge but it can never prove how it got there.

Every year, I teach a course on psychoanalytic theory and technique to graduate students in clinical psychology. In the first session, I try to engage the students in a lively way by asking them about how we know that there even is such a thing as the unconscious. Now, these are doctoral students trained in the ways of modern scientific psychology. They can be a bit constrained when it comes to imaginative thinking. But because this is an elective course they are not required to take, those who sign up often have some openness and curiosity about the deeper layers of the mind. So they are usually willing to play with the question and often come up with some pretty good answers.

The students' first response often involves the idea that we know about the unconscious through dreams. I once thought that this was an easy, textbook kind of answer, but I have come to believe that it is actually a more fascinating response than it might seem at first glance. After all, one could say that dreams are meaningless brain activity, a necessary physiological process to clear out the mental junk from the day. But we intuitively know that there is more to dreams than can be measured on an EEG machine. Dreams are personal. Dreams mean something.

Take, for example, the dream of a man in his first week of psychoanalysis. I heard about this case many years ago from one of my professors who used it as an illustration in one of his classes. (Please be advised that clinical material from actual patients is used sparingly throughout this book. Confidentiality and privacy have been protected by changing or omitting identifying information.) The patient was a mental health professional in his forties who had wanted to have an analysis for many years and felt that he really needed some help. But for a variety of reasons—some circumstantial and some of a yet-to-be-discovered psychological nature—he hadn't been able to bring himself to do it. He was very pleased to have the opportunity to begin therapy with my professor, a well-regarded female Kleinian analyst. The patient had studied Freud and Klein in school, so he felt he had an idea of what the process of analysis would be like and was eager to begin. In the second session, he shared the following dream:

> It was late at night and I was in bed; my wife and two children were asleep. I heard some noise in the bathroom, so I got up and went to check it out. I looked out the bathroom window and there was a woman on the roof, trying to break into the house. She was dressed in black with a hood over her face. It was clear that she was going to try to rob the house. I was terrified that she was going to harm my family. I cannot remember ever feeling so angry in my life. I reached through the window and grabbed the woman around the neck. I pulled her in and wrestled her to the floor. I was kicking her so hard that I thought I might actually kill her. But at some point, I realized that she was not fighting back.

She was telling me to stop. So I stepped back and pulled the hood off her face. I was shocked because the woman was a friend of mine from high school, a person I had liked but had not been particularly close to. Her name was Melanie.

Freud called dreams "the royal road to the unconscious," and if there was ever a royal road, this is it. I am hoping that the meaning of the dream is fairly obvious to you. It is a good teaching dream, because the elements are pretty straightforward. Even as students ourselves, when we heard the dream for the first time, my classmates and I were able to grasp some of its meaning.

If we keep the context in mind—that this is the very first dream in the very first week of therapy—would it be too much of a stretch to consider that the man is dreaming about his anxiety in beginning therapy? Can you see that he is letting us know that he is utterly terrified that the therapist (the black-hooded woman) will be a dangerous intruder, robbing him and hurting him in the most intimate and vulnerable of places (in the bathroom, potentially harming his family)? Can you see that his unconscious mind is revealing that he is going to fight against this intrusion with all his might? Perhaps this dream helps us understand why he put off therapy for so long, even though he consciously wished to have it and knew he needed it. Beneath the surface, he is frightened of what will be taken from him and of what will be done to him. He also might be frightened of what might be revealed about him—how aggressive and defensive he can become.

One of the most fascinating aspects about this story is that the patient was totally shocked by this dream and had no idea what it meant. He could not relate to his intense level of fear and aggressiveness, so out of character for him as he consciously knew himself at the time. He didn't link the dream to his attitudes about his new analyst, even with the marvelous tip-off that the intruder's name was Melanie. (Remember, the man had studied Klein, he knew that the analyst was Kleinian, and Klein's first name was Melanie. Dream symbols are often quite funny.) He didn't put together that he was dreaming about how frightened he was that the analyst would violently intrude into his psychic life and that he would fight against this intrusion to the edge of death. To me, the fact that he didn't have a clue about the meaning of the dream is another way of seeing this man's unconscious mind at work. Blind spots hide some of the deepest truths.

My professor told us that this man went on to have a turbulent but profitable analysis. He was open to his unconscious experience, and that proved to be a great help to him—once he got someone else to help him see what he couldn't see. That's really the key right there. *We need someone to help us see what we cannot see.*

The dream reveals one of the basic features of the unconscious mind. It is the receptacle for all of our unwanted, unbearable feelings and attitudes. What we hate about ourselves is buried there. What we fear about others is sent there. Our conflicts, our worries, our vulnerabilities, our hopes, and our terrors are relegated to the unconscious for safekeeping.

The trouble is that they are not really safe there. Our most intense feelings and fantasies need to be addressed. We have to face our fears. Otherwise, they become like Pandora's Box—all of the dangers are locked away in the unconscious mind, but like in a pressure cooker, they want to burst out. There is an enormous pressure for them to be revealed and expressed.

When we shut off these realities of our psychological life in the unconscious, they tend to leak out into conscious life. We are more aggressive than we intend to be. We are more depressed and withdrawn than we want to be. We soothe some unknown pain through food or sex or drugs or mindless activity. We run away without knowing what we are running from. We fail to succeed even when we try. Something holds us back. Something pushes us forward. It is like gravity—or, in this case, a trapped hurricane. There is a force that acts upon us that we cannot see.

If you remember the story of Pandora's Box, you know that it held not only the terrifying aspects of life; it also contained hope. So it is with the unconscious. The unconscious is the source of our passions, our creative energies, and our love of life. As I like to say, it is the gas in the engine; it is the juice that makes life worth living. If we rely on the unconscious too much as a dumping ground for unwanted parts of ourselves, we also lose contact with the most desirable, helpful, and hopeful parts of ourselves. In other words, if we use the unconscious to get rid of the bad, we get rid of the good stuff, too. Then we lose our drive to engage in life and to make meaning of our experiences.

Take as another example a set of dreams that a psychologist friend of mine, Lisa, had following her mother's death. Lisa was just turning forty when she lost her mother to a year-long battle with cancer. She and her mother had a relatively good relationship, having worked through the inevitable disappointments, hurts, and grievances that are part of any mother-daughter relationship. Grateful for all that her mother brought to her life, she grieved the loss of her mother deeply.

One evening over a glass of wine, Lisa told me four dreams that she had had in the weeks following her mother's death.

In the first dream, she dreamt that her mother had died and was walking down the long tunnel toward the light. Her mother turned to wave good-bye and saw that her daughter, my friend, was crying. Her mother said, "Sweetheart, don't worry about me. They'll have English muffins." Her mother loved English muffins.

A few days later, my friend had a second dream. She was a counselor in a girls' boarding school. Something was wrong with some of the girls and they needed her help. But it was pitch-black and she couldn't find her way to get to them. One of the administrators was there—a woman who had the same first name as her mother—but the woman was in such a deep sleep that she couldn't be woken up to help. Another helpful female figure was there, though. She was awake and alert and talking with Lisa. My friend said to her, "I can't find my stepping-stones. Where are my stepping-stones?"

And then, a few days later, she had a third dream. She was at work. For some reason, it was going to be her last day. So she went to her office to clean out her desk. Everything had been packed up, but she needed to clean out the drawers. And the main task was to sort through the silverware, as there were mismatched forks and knives and spoons, some of good quality and worth keeping (they'd fit with her set at home) and some to be thrown out.

And then Lisa told me the most recent dream that she had. She and her sister were young children, riding in the backseat of a car. The car was out of control, careening down a winding road. There was no one in the front seat. No one was driving. My friend's sister turned to her and said, "Hit the brakes!" And Lisa said, "My legs aren't long enough; I can't reach them."

Freud also referred to dreaming as "dream work," and here we can see my friend's unconscious mind working very hard to integrate and work through the loss of her mother. Lisa and I poured another glass of wine, grabbed some tissues, and talked for hours about this tender loss and what it would mean for her life.

I will leave most of the dream interpretation up to your own investigation and imagination, but I think it is plain to see some of the broad themes. Lisa was anxious about her mother's life after death; she was worried for her. And her unconscious mind sent her mother to a place of peace and rest. This is an act of integration with its acceptance of reality and a hope that the unknown will be a good place. This unconscious view of the afterlife—whether or not it is factually true—helps Lisa move on.

Even though, on one level, Lisa knew her mother was gone, the later dreams show that she is still not sure. Acceptance of this reality takes time and more work. In the dreams, Lisa is still looking for her mother. She is missing her. She needs her. She has to visit and revisit the reality that her mother is dead and gone; mother is in a deep sleep. A phase of Lisa's life (the job) is over; the maternal stepping-stones are missing; the mother who drives the car is no longer there. All of these images stand for Lisa's mother, and the hole that is left from her death must be mourned and then filled. The dreams point to the future: Lisa must find her own way, take and use the good psychological utensils her mother left her, and get in the driver's seat of her own life.

Perhaps you can see, then, how the unconscious is not just the source and receptacle of what is unwanted and unbearable. It is also the place where important psychological work is done. It is the place and the way in which we make meaning, make sense, and make peace. The work we do while we dream is deep work, for it helps us recognize what is most precious to us. If we can become more conscious of this unconscious work, we can use its wisdom to guide our lives. Psychoanalysis, of course, is uniquely designed to help us with this work. But good conversations with sensitive friends, as well as meditation, spiritual practices, reading good books, and personal reflection of all kinds, can help us, too.

In the first session with my students, we explore other ways we can see evidence of the unconscious in daily life—repetitive patterns in relationships, Freudian slips, the transmission of psychological difficulties from one generation to the next. If we start to look for the unconscious, we can see it. We just have to pay attention.

Inevitably, the seminar discussion turns to babies. If you have ever had a baby or spent much time with babies, you know from experience that babies come into the world with their own little personalities. We do not come into the world as blank slates. No two babies are the same. From the very beginning, we reach out to the world and engage it in a personally meaningful way. While the outside world has its impact in shaping us, inborn temperament has the first word to say on who we are and who we become. Each human being is as unique as a snowflake. And I suggest that at the heart of each little snowflake-personality is an unconscious inner world.

Consider this scenario. You have a group of newborn babies and each one had a reasonably good start in life. Normal pregnancies and deliveries, no complications, perfect Apgar scores. No fuss, no muss. They are all sleeping quietly in the nursery.

Suddenly, there is a loud noise. Someone has dropped a metal pan—crash, clatter, bang! The babies are all affected by the noise; they are disturbed out of their sleep. Why is it that a third of these healthy babies will gurgle, stretch, and fall right back to sleep? Why will another third wake up, begin to cry, and be comforted with modest effort by mother or caretaker and then fall back to sleep? And why will another third cry bloody murder, be inconsolable, and stay irritable for hours before they cry themselves into an exhausted slumber?

The answer is temperament. Yes, babies have personalities from the moment their little heads pop out into the world. We are preprogrammed to experience life in certain ways. Some of us are more sensitive than others. Some are more resilient. Some are shy, others outgoing. Some are more prone to aggression; others withdraw in the face of conflict and anxiety. Some lean more on intellect, others on emotion. Some hear a loud sound and shrug their shoulders, thinking, "Eh, no big deal." Others hear the same sound and say, "Oh my God! The world is coming to an end!"

The meaning we make from our experiences—even when we are mere babes—is what I have in mind when I say we each have an unconscious inner world. Even before our brains have developed fully, even before we have words, even before we can put two and two together, we are creating meaning. Take the three types of infants in our nursery scenario above. The quiet baby may have a sense that being in the world is a kind of numbing isolation or, better yet, a kind of ignorant bliss. The comforted baby may have some sense of safety in being held by a loving presence or, alternatively, a sense of self-confidence in being able to handle life's troubles. The inconsolable baby may suffer her way through life with a constant feeling of nameless dread, alone and threatened in a dangerous world. There is a kind of early, meaning-making process there—the beginnings of an unconscious psychological life.

Melanie Klein believed that our life in infancy has a powerful impact on how we develop into adults. She emphasized that it is not only our experiences that shape us, but the meaning we make of them. And what we take from our experiences has a lot to do with what we bring to them.

Remember Jacob and Esau from the Bible story? Jacob and Esau were the rivalrous twin sons of Isaac and Rebekah, descendants of Abraham in the patriarchal line of Israel. As the story goes, the twins were already fighting with each other in the womb. At the very point of birth, Jacob was grasping the heel of his one-minute-older brother as he slid through the birth canal, already showing signs of the competitiveness that would lead to such radical betrayal many years later. In the end, Jacob would steal his older brother's birthright, and the countries they would later lead would be at odds with each other for centuries. This is such a great example of what Klein meant when she said that our personalities have a trajectory from the beginning.

Now you may be skeptical, thinking this is just a story. How could a newborn—never mind a fetus—already have a personality? Believe it or not, we now have modern-day evidence to back it up. Alessandra Piontelli, an Italian psychoanalyst, did a fascinating set of studies observing the ultrasounds of twins in utero.[4] Studying the twins at several points during the mother's pregnancy, she found that the way they interacted in the womb—their relational style with one another, if you will—carried forward into how they related after birth and as they grew into more developed children. Our basic personalities are set more than we would like to believe they are.

If you had siblings or you have children, you know what I mean. Even if you look back at photos or videos of yourself as a young child, I'll bet you can see traces of the adult you have become. While our early experiences shape us, they only shape us so much. For example, if we pay attention to the differences between children in the same family, we can see that the same parents can be viewed by their children in different ways. One child might see his or her mother as loving and available, another might see her as overprotective and smothering, and yet another as stern and demanding. Even if we take into account factors such as birth order and changing circumstances, there is just something so compelling about the idea that our inborn personalities influence the meaning we make of our lives.

So how does environment come into play? As I like to say, while innate constitution may have the first word to say about who we become, it does not have the last. The way the world responds to our inborn predisposition shapes us—for better or worse. Jacob's envy was fueled by his mother playing favorites; Esau's naïve self-sufficiency was fueled by his father's blind loyalty. Instead of helping to rein in their sons' inborn rivalry, they encouraged it. Perhaps this is what it means for the sins of the parents to be visited on their children.

I think environment affects personality development like it affects intelligence. We are each born with some range of intellectual potential. With a rich environment—such as listening to Mozart in the womb, early creative stimulation, good nutrition, good schools, involved parents, and exposure to lots of different experiences that expand the mind—we develop toward the upper end of that range. But with an environment that lacks creative stimulation, proper nutrition, and parental involvement and care, we develop toward the lower end of that range. I think it is the same with the personality. An innately competitive child will grow up to be a competitive adult—but with positive influences, competitiveness can become a strength, and with negative influences, it can become a liability.

Certainly environment makes a difference. We can think of many examples. A particularly warm family experience can soften the sharp edges of a prickly porcupine temperament. A hostile and perfectionistic family experience can intensify that same predisposition. An abusive environment can weaken the resolve and resilience of even the most optimistic little personality, while a supportive, challenging environment can foster his or her great success in life. We are a blend of our psychological hardwiring and the software operating system of our early environment.

As we grow into adulthood, this lens helps us make sense of our experiences, but it also tends to distort them.

Perhaps you now have a sense of how I understand the development of the mind, how the internal and external worlds are constantly interacting with each other as we try to make sense of our experiences. Our unconscious expectations become a kind of filter through which we experience life for many years to come. As we grow into adulthood, this lens helps us make sense of our experiences, but it also tends to distort them. We think we are seeing the world as it really is, but actually we are seeing what the baby inside expects to see. And that is why we seem so insane sometimes. We are approaching our lives through the eyes of our baby selves, through the lens of unconscious reality.

As Buddha said, "Life is a creation of the mind."

A contemporary version of this idea adds a humorous twist: To paraphrase Albert Einstein, reality is only an illusion, although it is a very persistent one.

My thoughts about the unconscious mind are really a kind of introduction to all that is to come in the following chapters. They naturally lead to a critical question that I suspect is now on your mind. If the personality is so fixed and in such a state of confusion, how on earth can we ever hope to change?

CHAPTER TWO

IF YOU'RE NOT
MOVING FORWARD, YOU'RE
MOVING BACKWARD

On Growing

WHETHER YOU SUBSCRIBE TO THE theory of evolution, intelligent design, or creation, it is plainly evident that all living things are wired with the express purpose of surviving. Human beings are no different in this respect. We have a strong drive toward self-protection. We all know what it feels like to be galvanized by the instinct to flee or fight in the face of danger, whether that danger is physical or emotional. But we humans are unique among living things because we are also wired with the express purpose of growing psychologically. We have an innate urge to grow our minds by learning from and making meaning of our experiences.

There are other ways to describe this basic orientation to psychological development. Some would say that we are wired for love, which would seem to put the emphasis on the relational aspect of being human. I like that, too. We could say that human beings are wired for work, play, creativity, self-expression, generosity, and many other things. But, for me, *growing* seems to be a way of describing a central dynamic of human existence that encompasses all of these other aspects of life. And growing is what makes being alive so interesting, fulfilling, and challenging.

Growing is that aspect of life that pushes us beyond mere survival, even beyond adaptation—to become more than we need to be, to become more of what we want to be. It is that aspect of ourselves that motivates us to lean into life's challenges, even though we might be frightened or intimidated by them. People with a strong drive toward growth tend to live life with gusto. I am not talking about people who love bungee jumping, high-stakes gambling, or whirlwind transcontinental travel. In fact, I would describe myself as someone who has a strong drive for growing, and yet, as my sister says, I am *risk averse* when it comes to adventures like these. I prefer staying at a bed and breakfast over camping, and I like to play poker for M&M's rather than real money. What I am talking about is the human orientation toward development where love of learning and the desire to face life honestly, earnestly, and passionately win the day, more days than not. If you are a person well-endowed with the natural urge toward growth, then you know that curiosity, hard work, and learning through experience make life worth living.

This may sound pretty straightforward, but here's the rub: Sometimes—perhaps more often than we would like to admit— the urge toward survival is in direct conflict with the urge toward growth. This may not be readily apparent, since one would think that growing is simply the logical next step once you've got surviving down. But it is often not so. Growing fundamentally involves risk taking. It requires that one let go of that sense of security so essential to survival.

To use a very ordinary example, growing means taking off the training wheels from the bicycle. We lean into the potential of developing more independence and competence but must run the risk of falling over. Our safety is threatened. This challenging dynamic is at the heart of almost all of life. Often we prefer to play it safe by hiding out in what we know, rather than letting go and learning something new. It feels more secure to avoid change than to risk trying and failing. It feels smarter to keep our thoughts and feelings to ourselves than to share them in an intimate way.

While the balance between the urge toward survival and the urge toward growth varies from person to person, we all feel these tensions. At some level, we are all drawn to living in our bubbles and hiding under the proverbial covers, comfortable with what we know and protected from the dangers of what feels like a big, bad world out there. And yet, at the same time, we are drawn out of our bubbles by curiosity and a longing to engage.

Both Sigmund Freud and Melanie Klein believed that all people struggle with these two psychobiological forces—what they called the life and death instincts. The life instinct is that internal force that pushes us to grow and develop, to take risks so that we can be all that we can be. Here, growth is prized for the sense of satisfaction, enrichment, and deeper security that it brings. The death instinct is that force within that pulls us toward homeostasis. Here, self-protection is valued more highly than self-development. It is better to hide under the familiar rock and die than to venture out into the unknown world and be killed.

Think of Darwin's evolution of the species. Those species that survive over time are those that can engage the challenges of life—adapt, evolve, and develop ways to thrive despite obstacles.

Those species that become extinct are those that cannot adapt, those that shrink from life and wither away. Klein believed that all people have a relative balance between the life and death instincts, some leaning more toward growth and others leaning more toward self-protection.

———

Since you're reading this book, you must have some relative leaning toward the life instinct. Otherwise, you wouldn't bother. I have been concerned that some people would be turned off by the ideas in this book because they are too hard. I don't mean that what I am writing about is hard to understand, but the ideas are awfully hard to live. As I understand it, there is this fundamental truth about life: If you want to grow, you must take Robert Frost's "road less traveled." Or embrace the Buddha's principle of nonattachment. Or discover Jesus' narrow way. These wise ones all understood that a meaningful life is fundamentally about change. You've got to take up the cross and follow. I don't mean that you have to walk in their very footsteps, but that you have to get up and get going on your own way, knowing that hard work, determination, and sacrifice are inevitable parts of the process of growing.

If we are honest with ourselves, we have to admit that we don't like this idea at all. When the alarm clock goes off at 6:00 a.m., it is as if I am hardwired to hit the snooze button. For nine minutes (sometimes eighteen minutes), I give in to the death instinct. I want to stay in the womb, to cocoon in the warmth and protection of the blankets. I dread the day. I feel persecuted by its demands. I forget how much I love life and the satisfaction that it brings. And yet, soon after I rise, shower, and have my delicious coffee, I begin to wake up to the life instinct. Optimism, energy, and curiosity gain in strength. It is the inevitable rhythm of my morning. Each day, I must engage in this mini-struggle with the part of myself that wishes to shirk from life's challenges because I have temporarily lost contact with its many rewards.

I am always struck by this dynamic as it plays itself out in an ordinary way between fitness trainer and client at the local gym. Have you ever watched (or ever been) the client who whines throughout her workout, complaining to her trainer, "Why do you make me lift such heavy weights?" Or, better yet, "Why do you always make me sweat?" It is a frustrating yet rather hilarious moment when one realizes that one cannot get the benefit of the workout without the strain, that— in fact—one has intentionally put oneself in that position in order to grow. Deep down, we know that the saying is true—no pain, no gain— but that doesn't mean we have to like it!

Resistance to growth is something that we don't like to recognize in ourselves, yet in many ways it is essential to acknowledge if one really wants to grow.

Resistance to growth is something that we don't like to recognize in ourselves, yet in many ways it is essential to acknowledge if one really wants to grow. The reality of resistance to growth explains why so many of us try to change but cannot. In Romans 7:15, the Apostle Paul speaks about this common problem when he writes,

"I do not understand my own actions. For I do not do what I want, but I do the very thing I hate." Many of us relate to this frustrating experience. However, when we can step back to acknowledge it as Paul did, we gain a valuable perspective. We begin to see how we actually contribute to our own troubles, fueling the fire rather than doing what we can to put it out.

It takes a lot of effort for us to grow because, as we can tell from observing ourselves, we human beings tend to unconsciously invest, over and over, in supporting the status quo, even if it is problematic. Freud called this *the repetition compulsion,* a highly charged dynamic in our inner worlds that keeps us trapped in vicious circles, making the same mistakes, hitting the same dead ends, and backing ourselves into the very corners we are trying to get out of. The conscious voice says, "I want to change!" and yet the unconscious voice says, "It is too dangerous! Keep doing what you know. You haven't died yet." This unconscious train of thought shows one of the key reasons why we resist change: We are afraid of dying.

Now that may sound a bit dramatic, but the inner world is populated by some rather dramatic characters, the first and foremost being our baby selves. While the most adult part of our personalities might have good judgment and motivation for dealing with reality—and might be quite invested in growing—there is a central part of the personality that, just like an infant, comes into the world frightened, needy, and 100 percent dependent on another person for its survival. In a very real sense, there is a baby self within each of us that fears for its life. This is the starting point of personality development. The baby self, having no sense of time, lives on as if it were living in the first and most vulnerable days of life.

I hope you find this metaphor as helpful as I do. I think it is a good alternative to the old metaphor of the psyche being like a wild horse (the id) that needs to be tamed and bridled (the super-ego) by a strong rider (the ego). I can relate better to the contemporary depiction of the psyche being more like an internal family in which internal parents work to help comfort, feed, discipline, and raise an internal baby, because it feels so much closer to my experience. I know I have a baby part of my personality that can get cranky, confused, irrational, and impulsive and needs the help of my more grown-up self. I also know I have a baby part that is curious, playful, and creative, and wants to learn more about this fascinating world of ours and wants to become more capable of handling it. So many of the psychological forces of life come from this baby part of the personality. I have found that getting to know and having a good relationship with her is key to being well and living well.

But if you find it hard to picture yourself having an inner world that is populated with internal babies of all ages, as well as internal parents trying to have relationships with them, try to start thinking about it in another way. Picture the psyche as a tree trunk. All the layers of the self, through all the times and seasons of our lives, are preserved inside—alive—like rings in the trunk of a tree. The core of that tree trunk holds a lot of power, both in the beginning and throughout our lives. Being the oldest part of self, it also has a lot of influence because we have been relying on it for so long.

The core of the tree trunk is the baby part of the self, the center of the personality. I like to call it the baby-core of the personality. Put simply, we are often unknowingly responding more to the baby-core's needs and demands than to the needs and demands of the outer layers, or "adult" part of our personalities.

So, if you can allow yourself to engage with this vivid metaphor about the baby-core of the personality, you might ask, "What is such an infant to do if she wants to survive?" As you can guess from what I've been sharing so far, one approach is that she can give in to the death instinct and try to flee from danger. That is, she can use the approach of *avoidance*. Kleinian analysts call it "getting unborn" or "becoming an unborn baby." You can try to stay in the womb (metaphorically speaking) forever. Avoid risk at all costs, underachieve, hide out. This approach is something that we are all prone to using, at least from time to time, and I see it more and more in young people today. I call it "failure to launch," borrowing the term from a romantic comedy. These are the twenty-eight-year-olds still living with overprotective moms and dads, sheltered from the dangers of life and falsely convinced that they can have all of the goodies in life without getting born into the world and growing up.

The problem with the approach of avoidance is expressed in the simple truth of the adage that if you're not moving forward, you're moving backward. To further develop the gym analogy, we all know that muscle, if not exercised, will atrophy. If you sit on the couch long enough (for example, playing video games or surfing the Internet), you're going to have some problems—with your body and your mind. This is the place where a vicious circle can get set in motion. Our confidence deteriorates the more we avoid facing life's difficulties. The less we face life, the less capable we feel. And the less capable we feel, the less we try. We can't get up off the couch. If we're not moving forward, we're moving backward.

While the couch potato analogy is a good one to understand the cost of avoidance, it doesn't really capture the severity of the problems that tend to arise. I try to highlight this with my patients, as vividly as possible, by describing avoidance as leading to the Mold Effect. They usually cringe when they hear it described in this way—as they should. Living things, left alone in the darkness, tend to grow bad stuff. If you are so afraid of the dangerous world out there that you hide from it, you will be left alone with your fears—and fears, like mold, multiply when unattended. The only real way to diminish your fears is to face them.

The other popular approach used to cope with fears of dying in the face of life's dangers is *denial*. We can pretend that we are not afraid at all. Melanie Klein put a finer point on this approach by calling it *manic denial*. The manic part of manic denial is an illusion that we can cleverly conjure about ourselves (unconsciously, of course). In our minds, we can puff ourselves up, imagining that we are as invulnerable, invincible, and masterful as Superman himself. You can see the magic in this way of thinking, as needs, fears, and limitations disappear in the blink of an eye. Manic denial is such a common approach to coping with life that I am going to devote a whole chapter to it, but for now, let me give you a preview of coming attractions.

In our culture, we find a well-known and accessible depiction of the use of manic denial in the story of Peter Pan. The psychology of the story is so classic that psychologists have even coined a term to describe it: the Peter Pan Syndrome. It is the story of a little boy who never grew up because he didn't want to. Instead, he created an imaginary world run by children without any parents. He tried to deny his need for parents by living out the fantasy that he could have all of the benefits of being a grown-up without the hard work that growing up involves.

I offer the story of Peter Pan as an example of how we often use manic denial to cope with the anxiety of being babies: We masquerade as grown-ups. The details of the story say it all. First, Peter denies his smallness—he is arrogant, boastful, grandiose, and as full of himself as any little egomaniac could be. Then he denies his need for his parents—as one version of the story goes, when Peter was an infant, he abandoned his parents for the crime of having another baby. If that's not enough, he denies reality— simply by thinking "happy, wonderful thoughts," he can fly! And, above all, he denies his fear of dying—he is always putting himself in harm's way, appearing fearless and cocky, even to the point of saying, "To die would be an awfully big adventure!"

Peter Pan is an archetype, a kind of character who speaks to us about ourselves. He does not want to face his vulnerability, his need, and even his desire to grow up, so he pretends he can rise above it all. He lives out the fantasy that Neverland is so wonderful that he could not imagine ever leaving.

Despite the exciting tone of J. M. Barrie's incredible tale, beneath the surface there are rumblings of a more vulnerable, tender reality that cannot be denied. If we pay close attention to the story, we see Peter, at least now and then, revealing that he feels uncomfortable, lonely, and afraid. Beneath his bravado, he is constantly anxious and worried about being haunted by crocodiles and Captain Hook. When offered a chance for a real childhood back in London, for a brief instant, he considers going back with the Darling children to a real mother and father. Though he tries to cover it up, we know that he has no real peace of mind.

Because of Peter's denial, we can only see glimpses and make assumptions about what is going on in his inner world; we see through the cracks for only a moment. But the other characters in the story are more in contact with the breadth of feelings in their lives, both wonderful and dreadful. In other words, they are more whole. If you know the story, you might remember the eldest child, Wendy, with her strong maternal instinct, concern, and fierce judgment. Or her brothers, John and Michael, with their fears of flying and fighting, along with their desire to go home. And who could forget Tinkerbell, with her jealousy and protectiveness?

For me, one of the most touching images in the story is that of the Lost Boys—Peter Pan's "gang"—a group of boys who lost their parents, were snatched from their baby carriages, never to be found again. The Lost Boys seem to represent a good, wholesome relationship between children and their parents, offering an alternative to the relationship that is so twisted and turned around in Peter's character. According to Peter, children have no need for parents, so he is not a lost boy at all. And while he tries to peddle this propaganda to the Lost Boys, they do not believe it for too long. Deep down, the Lost Boys are able to stay in touch with the painful loss of their parents—whom they love and on whom they depend. They know they are lost and they jump at the chance to have parents again.

This dynamic was touchingly portrayed in the stage version of the play I saw a few years ago in Los Angeles. I welled up with tears at the moment when the Lost Boys decide to go back to London with Wendy and her brothers, and they joyfully sing, "A mother, a mother, we finally have a mother!" They embrace the very longing that Peter sadly must deny. It is sad because he cannot really experience the joys of love, dependency, and growing up. And it is sad because he is left to fight his battles alone, battles that will never be won but only perpetuated for all of time. By not facing his own anxieties in the realm of the real world, he can never defeat them or be free of them.

While the resistances to growth are tricky and powerful, they can be managed if one understands and faces the underlying factors. If you are following closely, you can see that one of the main factors that must be dealt with is anxiety. When it comes to resistance, it is a frightened baby who is running the show. We each need to develop a good relationship with that inner baby, so that she can be less frightened and learn how to face her fears. By facing our fears, we have the opportunity to grow up and, in so doing, experience the satisfactions of love, inner security, and peace of mind.

In February of 2006, I had the good fortune to attend a worship service celebrating the fortieth anniversary of the Graduate School of Psychology at Fuller Theological Seminary, my alma mater. Dr. John Ortberg, also an alumnus, preached a moving sermon about the essential aspects of growing. To an audience of Christian therapists, he spoke poetically and pointedly about the joys and frustrations of helping people change, about how meaningful it is to be part of their healing process, and how difficult the work can be. His sermon was centered on three essential features of the growing process—a formula that he borrowed from another well-known Christian therapist, Dr. Henry Cloud.[5] I had never heard of Cloud's "essential ingredients of growth" and was deeply moved to hear them delivered by such an insightful speaker as Dr. Ortberg.

Ortberg began by talking about the first two ingredients—grace and truth. He described grace in the traditional Christian way as "unmerited favor," and by this he meant that we human beings really need to have an engaged, nonjudgmental support team available if we are to do the hard work of growing. I take this to be true for the inner world as well as the outer world. We need parents, siblings, and friends in our external and internal worlds to be there for us, to encourage us to get out of bed, to get born into the world, and to face our anxieties. Grace has a special place in the Christian understanding of growth, too, for here God at God's best is seen as our chief supporter and most loving, forgiving parent.

But Ortberg went on to say that grace alone is not sufficient; we also must engage with the truth. He used the concept of truth in the same way that I am using the concept of reality. We must face the truth about ourselves; we must deal with reality as it is. I love that he promoted the idea that God is fundamentally on the side of the truth. I think that reflects a view of God at God's best too—not a magician taking us away from the problems of the world, but a parent who lovingly holds us accountable to facing the truth about ourselves. It is the combination of grace and truth that is so essential, for grace without truth would never lead to substantial change. And truth is nearly impossible to face without grace, for it is too hard and too painful, and so we wish to avoid it.

I would have been quite satisfied if Ortberg had stopped there. I would have left the worship service feeling like he had spoken about something substantial in the psychological and spiritual journey. I would have felt that he had validated an approach that I had understood and tried to practice in my life and work. But he went one step further. The next step was such a wonderful surprise, it made me gasp. I'm not kidding. He said that there are three essential ingredients to lasting change and growth: grace, truth, and . . . time.

I exclaimed to myself silently, "Time!" That's the ingredient we so often wish to leave out. That's the bit that cannot be left out. It's the secret to yeast, to a good marinade, to fine wine. It is the key to making a lasting and deep love relationship, to fighting an illness, to grieving the loss of a loved one, to maturing in faith, to making peace, and to growing up.

In the presence of someone who is struggling, it is a common, sympathetic response to say, "It just takes time." That is a lovely sentiment, but it is not quite the whole truth. It does not *just* take time. It takes grace and truth, too. But it does take time.

So let us ask the next question. Why does growing take so much time? It is an understandable question, after all. I often ask it. My patients often ask it. We are in good company, because even physicians in Freud's day asked him the same question. Freud tells the story of a colleague who once wrote to him, saying, "What we need is a short, convenient, outpatient treatment for obsessional neurosis." Freud commented, "I could not supply him with it and felt ashamed; so I tried to excuse myself with the remark that specialists in internal diseases, too, would probably be very glad of a treatment for tuberculosis or carcinoma, which combined these advantages."[6] Growth in psychoanalysis mirrors growth in life; it takes more time than we expect.

But why does it take so much time? Growing takes time for two main reasons. The first is that there are many forms of resistance to growing. In the body, resistance to healing is a particularly thorny problem in treating tuberculosis and cancer. Confused, the body fights against its best interests, even against the treatment itself. The same is true of the life of the mind. We get in our own way. Mostly out of fear, we maintain the status quo and turn away from change. All of this resistance has to be worked through and, bit by bit, overcome. One of my patients once told me of a sculpture of Sisyphus, pushing his boulder up the mountain, just as the story goes. But this sculpture added a new dimension to the image. There, on the other side of the boulder, was another Sisyphus, pushing the same boulder back down the mountain. We work against ourselves.

The other reason that growth takes so much time is because that is simply how it is. That is reality. That is how we human beings are wired. This is an essential part of reality that we must make peace with, and it is a hard one. A story that illustrates this point is an episode from *The Brady Bunch* television show. In using it I know that I date myself, but I happily grew up on that show and, all these years later, I can see how many wonderful psychoanalytic lessons can be found in its stories. This particular episode stands out to me as a great illustration of the reality that growing takes time, even under the best of circumstances.

Poor Bobby, the youngest of the three brothers, is painfully overtaken with envy that Peter and Greg are so much bigger, taller, stronger, and smarter than he is. So he tries to take a shortcut in the process of growing. The boys have an exercise high bar over the doorway to their bedroom. Bobby grabs hold of it and hangs on, for hours, hoping that he will be able to speed the process of growing by stretching out and getting taller. This is an image we can all relate to, even though it is quite ridiculous. It is ridiculous because we all know that you cannot speed up the process of growth. It is also hilarious because, even if it worked, he wouldn't be taller—his arms would just be longer!

Growing takes time. As someone once said to me, the only way to grow is to eat your Wheaties. All we can do is do all we can do to make the conditions optimal so that growth can take place. We need grace—the committed love and support of others. We need truth—the experience of facing ourselves and our lives, *exactly as they are*. And we need time—time to face all that we resist and then to let the natural process of growth unfold.

We must face ourselves, as we are, with all of our limitations, anxieties, unconscious maneuvers, hopes, and capabilities.

Wilfred Bion, a revolutionary psychoanalyst who followed Melanie Klein, coined a phrase that best captures the approach to growing that works: "learning through experience." We must engage life, not turn away from it. We must make mistakes, risk and fail, and try again. We must face ourselves, as we are, with all of our limitations, anxieties, unconscious maneuvers, hopes, and capabilities. We must contend with both life and death instincts, side by side, in tension with each other and in a strange kind of cooperation with each other. And we need to make good use of our parents—both internal and external—so that we can build on the resources we have been given. For we human beings were designed not only to survive but to grow and develop, to become more than we need to be, more of what we want to be.

While growing is difficult, it is also one of the aspects of life that is most valuable and meaningful. Philosopher Alan Watts described it as the essential nature of the universe. The perishability and changefulness of the world are part of what makes it so beautiful. Its elusiveness is part of its charm, of its liveliness and its loveliness. Embracing the dynamic process of growth brings a sense of competency, depth, and peace that cannot be gained in any other way.

I found a greater appreciation of this reality when, in my twenties, I went through a period of anxiety as I contemplated what heaven would be like. The picture I had, based on my traditional Christian upbringing, was that heaven would be a place of perfection, where there would be no more tears or crying, where the streets would be paved with gold, where we would have no need for anything because we would be completely satisfied with ourselves and at one with God. I have to admit that, at the time, I had a very peculiar response to that picture: It worried me.

Even in those naïve, youthful years, I had a sense that the best thing about life was growing, even if it meant there would be pain and suffering. I realized that my picture of heaven did not allow any room for that kind of growth. Growing involves anxiety, risk, and a sense of being incomplete. I did not want to be deprived of that kind of experience, even in heaven. It took me a while to work out another way of viewing heaven, and I had to look for concepts outside of my Christian upbringing. I don't know who suggested it first, but there is the idea out there that heaven is whatever you want it to be. If you love tulips, your heaven will be filled with them. If you love heavy metal music, your heaven will reverberate with it. If you love English muffins, your heaven will serve them for breakfast every day. I kind of liked that idea. So I decided that if my heaven is imperfect, because imperfection makes room for growing, then so be it. I wouldn't have it any other way.

CHAPTER THREE

HARD WORK GROWS THE MIND

On Work

AS I THINK ABOUT THE process of psychological growth, I really like the three-ingredient recipe of grace, truth, and time. But I also realize that there is one part of the recipe that hasn't yet been highlighted. It's so obvious that it's easy to overlook, like having a list of ingredients for a delicious soup but not mentioning that you have to put them together in a saucepan, turn the heat on, simmer, and stir. Yes, psychological growth takes grace, truth, and time. But it also takes work.

While I do believe that we have a natural, built-in inclination to grow, I don't think it just happens. Psychological growth is actually an achievement. You have to work for it. Because such growth involves reaching beyond our comfort zone, it means we have to overcome another inclination in life that is even more basic in our personalities. It is the primitive orientation to seek pleasure and avoid pain. That's where we all begin.

We start with a basic formula. Freud called it the *pleasure-pain principle*. If it feels good, then eat it, take it, or do it. If it feels bad, then spit it out, get rid of it, or avoid it. This principle works pretty well for most living creatures, and even organisms as simple as bacteria use it to survive. For a little while, it works pretty well for people, too. During the first few months of our lives—when life is uncomplicated and all we need to do is eat, pee, poop, and sleep—the pleasure-pain principle is a winning strategy. Smile and coo if it feels good; frown and scream bloody murder if it feels bad. In either case, Mom will come running, and all will be well.

The trouble for us humans, though, is that the pleasure-pain principle has its limitations. We cannot always get immediate access to pleasure. We cannot always get immediate relief from pain. At first and for a rather long while, we are utterly dependent on someone else to provide our pleasure and relieve our pain for us. And despite our wishes and demands, Mom cannot always be there at the instant we need her. She is only human, after all. She is a separate person. Even the best multitasker in the world can't do everything all at once. Sometimes Mom has to attend to her own needs and the needs of others. Even when she is right there with us, sometimes it takes her a little while to figure out exactly what it is that we need. All of this means that we have to cope with the demands of reality. And that's where the work comes in.

You see, reality interferes with the pleasure-pain principle. It calls upon us to deal with the inevitable pains and frustrations of life. It propels us into growth.

Freud called the capacity to cope with life's challenges the *reality principle*. He believed that psychological maturity comes as we turn toward the realties of life rather than turning away from them. We must leave the pleasure-pain principle behind if we are to grow our minds.

We human beings have the potential to shape and grow our lives in extremely productive ways. But we have to work for it. The mind needs to be developed, and the only way it can be developed is to be challenged. Like the body, the mind needs to be exercised in order to get stronger. And the way the mind is exercised is by taking on painful, confusing, and frustrating experiences and building the capacity to deal with them.

In her exercise videos, Jane Fonda took the popular saying "no pain, no gain" to a new level. There's profound psychoanalytic wisdom in that phrase. We've got to push ourselves to get stronger. We've got to carry more weight, go a longer distance, and reach beyond our limits. Sometimes it will make us sore. Sometimes it will be painful. But it is the only way to grow our mental and emotional capacity so that we can better deal with the challenges of life.

. . . the way the mind is exercised is by taking on painful, confusing, and frustrating experiences and building the capacity to deal with them.

Another way of depicting this kind of psychological work is seeing it like developing a thicker skin. If you are familiar with playing a stringed instrument, you know what I mean. Guitarists and violinists need to develop calluses on their fingers if they're going to play for very long. They need the friction of skin against string to develop a foundation for playing well. The pain these musicians experience at first is necessary in order to strengthen the skin on their fingers so that they can play with less pain in the future. Athletes and dancers know about this, too. And let's not forget about hikers, woodworkers, and farmers. They all have worked through their share of blisters-that-hurt to build calluses-that-protect. By engaging in the roughness of their craft, they develop physical toughness, strength, and endurance that actually make engaging in their particular craft or skill easier in the long run.

The mind is much like the body in this respect. We must push ourselves to get mentally tough, too. In upcoming chapters, I'm going to explore all sorts of mental strengths that we can develop to help us be more successful in life. For now, I want to highlight two of the most important capacities: delaying gratification and bearing frustration. Where seeking pleasure and avoiding pain are the yin of life, delaying gratification and bearing frustration are the yang.

The pleasure-seeking baby's approach to his imagined world is "I need it. I want it. I get it." But as the reality of life punctures the magic of his fantasy, the baby learns the universal truth consistent with the title of the Rolling Stones song: "You can't always get what you want." Reality shows us that we can't just ring a bell and have a butler serve up pleasure on a silver platter whenever we please. Sometimes we have to wait. Sometimes we have to work for it. This is what the capacity to delay gratification is all about. It is one of the keys to a mature and satisfying life.

A person who can commit to working without immediate rewards has the opportunity to grow something really substantial over time. This is true for a lot of valuable experiences in life, like schooling, parenting, developing a career, and, of course, being in therapy. Take retirement investing, for example. If you can approach investing as a long-term project, patiently waiting through the ups and downs in the financial markets, investing steadily as you go—you have the chance to build something of much greater value than the pleasure-seeking day trader. This is a great metaphor for psychological life. If we can turn toward the challenges of reality, invest the best we can, hang in there, wait it out, and not give up, we get to truly understand the last line of that Stones song, "But if you try sometimes you just might find you get what you need."

The pain-avoiding baby's approach to the bad stuff in life is "Get rid of it. Get rid of it all. Get rid of it now." There is no mind in this approach. When the baby sniffs out that pain is around the corner, her knee-jerk reaction is evacuation. GET RID OF IT! As I like to say, it is impulse to action with nothing in between. Rather than growing the mind, however, the pain-avoiding approach has the opposite effect. It weakens the mind. If we instantly get rid of our pain—through projection, denial, and other kinds of wishful maneuvers—we never learn to cope with it.

Developing the capacity to bear frustration means that we take our frustrations and try to work with them. We add a middle step between impulse and action. We feel our pain, and we think about it. Rather than giving up, we stay with it. We bear it. We tolerate it. To put it simply, we hang in there. When you really think about it, these capacities to bear painful emotions are a rather remarkable psychological achievement.

Look at it from the point of view of the baby. When we are angry with Mom for not being there when we need her, we can turn away and give up on her. We can withdraw like a turtle into its shell. But there's a consequence to that strategy. We foreclose on any help we might have received had we stayed open and available.

On the other hand, if we can muster up the psychological strength to stay engaged with Mother even though she is frustrating us, we give ourselves a much better chance of being helped by her at some point in the (hopefully) near future. If we can bear the frustration of Mother's absence, then we can still cry out and reach out to her, letting her know that we need her. This means we are able to maintain a relationship with her, despite feeling upset with her. If we can bear these sorts of frustrations, then we also can let her tend to us when she returns. And that attitude makes all the difference in the world. It means we are still in the game.

There's nothing like watching a professional tennis player or a basketball team that loses a big lead to know how these mental capacities make or break us. So much of success in sports—and, frankly, in life itself—is mental. Beyond the physical training, we've got to dig deep to play the mental game well, too. This means that we must work to develop the kind of mind that can cope under pressure, the kind of mind that can get in the game and stay in the game even when we are losing our lead, and just when we want to give up. That kind of mind can only be developed in the crucible of challenging experiences. If we want to learn to stand the heat, we've got to get into the kitchen.

Wilfred Bion thought a lot about Freud's idea of the pleasure-pain and reality principles. This is where his idea of "learning through experience" comes in. When we face frustration rather than evade it, he said, we develop *"mental muscle."* I love that image. Just as we must challenge the body to develop physical muscle, so must we challenge the mind to develop mental muscle. It cannot happen in a vacuum. It cannot happen without pain. It cannot happen in Nirvana. It only happens when we take on difficult experiences and learn from them.

Hard work grows the mind.

When we are guided by the reality principle, we develop a deeper capacity to deal with life more effectively. What was once difficult is now easier. What once frightened us now feels familiar. Life becomes more manageable. And there's something even deeper that we gain. Because we can see that we have grown stronger, we have greater confidence that we can grow stronger still. This is the basis of feeling *capable*, which I think is the wellspring of a satisfying life.

We could learn a thing or two about how to improve our teaching methods from this simple understanding of the development of the mind. Sadly, teaching methods have become more about the pleasure-pain principle than the reality principle. Students want to get through their classes rather than learn something in them. Teachers are encouraged to go easy on their students and are criticized for being too strict, giving tough feedback, or pushing students to really think. Parents are so worried about their children's future that they sometimes give in to the temptation to do their kids' school projects for them. The whole system colludes with this pleasure-pain principle mind-set, even though, at some level, we know that the path of least resistance leads to suffering for everyone.

It's not easy to take the less-traveled road. After all, teachers are evaluated by the performance of their students on standardized tests. Students must get good grades to get into a good college, right? As a result, modern education has become more about flash cards, memorization, and teaching to the test. We understand the pressure to toe the company line. We are sympathetic. But still, it is no wonder that our children are having such trouble finding their way into adulthood.

On the other hand, when teaching methods engage the mind, real learning takes place—the kind of learning that takes root and lasts. This is the kind of learning that builds character and grows the mind. The teachers we remember are those who inspired us. They are the teachers who got into both our heads and our hearts. They motivated us to engage with reality and made us think, digest, wrestle, and grapple with life's complexities. Hopefully, at some point during our education, we had a teacher, like the Robin Williams character in the movie *Dead Poets Society*, who possessed the courage to throw caution to the wind, to stand on a desk— literally or metaphorically—and inspire and encourage us to embrace life and find our passion.

Do you remember that greeting card I had on the bulletin board over my desk? The one that listed Ten Things to Make Besides Money? Make love, make peace, make amends, make do, etc. This is the reality principle in living color. If we want to have something of real value in our lives, we have to make it. It doesn't just magically appear. It cannot be fed to us on a spoon. It doesn't happen by osmosis. We have to seize it. We have to make it ourselves.

As I said, psychological growth is an achievement. This means that we must move beyond the pleasure-pain principle and take responsibility for our lives. We have to work for it.

But this is easier said than done. As Buddhist monk Bhante Henepola Gunaratana puts it, "The reason we are all stuck in life's mud is that we ceaselessly run from our problems and after our desires."[7] So pointed, so true. So often, we look down on work. We turn up our noses at effort. We want to have an easy life in which everything is done for us. The inner baby feels entitled to have all of her needs met— right here, right now, just the way she wants it. We want to be bathed in sensual pleasure, to feel comfy, cozy, and happy all the time. Sometimes my patients feel such resentment about being challenged to work so hard in their treatment that they ask, "Can't I just have a cookie?"

We don't realize that the challenges of life are gifts, opportunities for growth.

We don't realize that the challenges of life are gifts, opportunities for growth. We don't understand that we cannot feel good in the depths of our being unless we work, grow, and deal with the challenges of life. Instead, we have the mistaken idea that we will feel good about ourselves if we are taken care of, pampered, and adored. We call it unconditional love and believe it is our birthright. We do not realize that when little princes and princesses are worshipped and spared from hard work, they tend to turn into spoiled brats rather than well-adjusted citizens of this world.

So it takes some doing to learn this counterintuitive lesson that work—rather than the absence of it—is what brings pleasure in the deepest sense. We benefit greatly when our parents understand that the best thing they can do for us is help us learn how to do for ourselves. This is difficult for many parents in American society today. There is an innate protective urge that parents feel for their children. We want to spare them pain. We want to protect them from danger. All of these motivations have their place, but only in moderation, for if we keep our children in a protective bubble, they do not have the experiences they need to develop the kind of thick skin necessary to do well in life. If we really want them to be happy, we have to nudge them out of the nest.

Self-esteem and self-confidence are developed through a combination of loving parental support and personal success in facing life's challenges. We may idealize an easy life, but in reality it is of little use to us, even if it were possible. We feel capable only when we do difficult things, when we face life's challenges rather than run away from them. If we are protected from these sorts of challenges, we wither away. If we are urged and equipped to face them, we become stronger.

Can you relate to this idea? Do you ever stop to soak in the pleasure of your accomplishments, even the most basic ones? Do you feel good when you pay your bills on time? Do you have a sense of pride after a difficult conversation that you feel you handled well? Do you feel satisfied when you try something new— even if it doesn't work out perfectly, but just because you had the courage to try? Do you feel a sense of accomplishment when you finish a project, clean your house, kick ass in an exercise class, give a good speech, or solve a thorny problem? These are the sorts of experiences that really build self-esteem from the inside. Taking care of business is the foundation for a mature character. It may not always be pleasant, and it surely will not be free of pain, but it offers a chance to build good feelings that last.

Bhante Gunaratana goes on: "View all problems as challenges. Look upon negativities that arise as opportunities to learn and to grow. Don't run from them, condemn yourself, or bury your burden in saintly silence. You have a problem? Great. More grist for the mill. Rejoice, dive in, and investigate."[8]

Freud couldn't have said it better.

It is important to get this orientation toward work straightened out, because a lot of people have it backward. In fact, that's where most of my patients begin. They think that it is better to avoid pain than to face it. And if they can avoid pain and feel pleasure, then all the better.

A prime example of this approach to living is addiction. So many manifestations of addiction are about decreasing pain and increasing pleasure. Whether it is addiction to sex, food, work, gambling, alcohol, or other drugs, those struggling with addiction often are trying to get away from facing the pain of life and replace it with good feelings. The addict often begins as a regular Joe or Jane who is just trying to relax, trying to get some relief from a troubled relationship, stress at work, financial pressures, or even physical pain. But for some people, the drive toward pleasure and away from pain intensifies to the point where connections to reality and the mind are temporarily lost.

Alcohol, opiates, and certain other drugs have powerful effects on both the body and the mind that are difficult to resist. They slow down the whole system, relaxing and relieving it from distress. This state is something that every human being longs for, at a deep level. But if we seek to maintain that blissful state exclusively, we undermine our success in life because we are turning away from reality rather than learning how to cope with it. In other words, used in excess, all forms of addiction evoke a kind of anti-reality principle. Rather than turning toward reality, the addict turns away. Rather than being alive to real life, the addict seeks to deaden any awareness of it. We hear echoes of this dynamic in the slang terms that are used for excessive substance use. Wasted, trashed, bombed. The addict's unconscious aim is to destroy mindfulness, to throw away any awareness of the troubles that he or she would otherwise have to face.

One of the quintessential challenges of addiction is that it is not only opposed to psychological growth, it is opposed to thinking at all. It is an attack on the mind itself. This is why we see so much *denial* at the heart of addiction—and why recovery is so difficult. The very resource that is most needed for recovery—the mind itself, with its awareness of reality—has been trashed, thrown in the garbage heap.

One of the reasons why the twelve-step programs (Alcoholics Anonymous, Narcotics Anonymous, Gamblers Anonymous, etc.) have been so central to recovery from addiction is that they are based on the fundamental awareness that the adult mind of the person suffering from addiction has been lost. These programs emphasize that the addict must acknowledge that he has returned to the powerlessness and utter dependency of infancy. Without an adult mind of his own with which to think about his life and cope with it, he desperately needs the help of others and a power greater than himself.

The concept of surrender to a higher power has been so essential in recovery efforts because it is based in deep psychological truths. For example, Step Twelve describes a spiritual awakening, a kind of rebirth that dovetails with the psychoanalytic ideas we are exploring. The addict must go back to the beginning; or rather, he must come to the realization that he has already gone back to the beginning. He must recognize his need for a mother. Whether that mother is God or some other way of understanding him or her, he must find a power and strength greater than himself on which to rely. Forgive me if this sounds trite, but the addict must be born again.

In recovery from addiction, a person must go back to the beginning in a proper sense. He must take a second chance at engaging in a process of growth guided by the reality principle. It is not difficult to see the values of the reality principle in each and every one of the twelve steps of these remarkable programs. There is nothing like making a searching and fearless moral inventory (as in Step Four) to get you turned toward life and its many realities. And few things strengthen conviction to recovery more than the hard, painstaking work of making amends (as in Step Nine). Bit by bit, step by step, the addict must face life on life's terms.

One of the saving graces in psychological life is that if you take the time to study reality, you find that it is actually more pleasant to deal with it rather than to avoid it. Ask any addict who knows what it means to hit rock bottom. The reality principle just works better. If you have the courage to take on difficult experiences, you discover that it becomes easier to take them on. Living life on life's terms does involve pain, but avoidance brings the true suffering.

There are two types of work in life. Maybe you could call them two levels of the reality principle. The first is to face what comes to you in life. The second is to seek to take on even more.

Most people are doing well if they can get into the mode of facing life as it comes. That is challenge enough. Ordinary life requires effort. There is laundry to be done, money to manage, food to prepare, a home to keep organized, a car to maintain, a leaky sink to repair. Add school or a job to that and you have deadlines, projects, dicey situations, and stressful relationships that need your effort and attention. If you are a parent, there are kids who need to be washed and fed, helped with homework, transported to and from any number of places and/or events, listened to, disciplined, played with, rescued from killing their little brothers. Then there's the dog, the taxes, the friendships, the parents, the partner, the personal needs. You've got to make it to the gym, eat better, tend to your sex life, and figure out which candidate to vote for in the next election.

Dealing with the demands of real life in a healthy manner requires discipline, mindfulness, and balance. And that's when life is going relatively smoothly. But life doesn't always go relatively smoothly. It throws more at us, often through no fault of our own. Your mother gets Alzheimer's. You get laid off. Your husband gets injured. Your best friend dies of cancer. You have a child with special needs. The stock market crashes. Your rent is jacked up. Life comes at you without mercy.

Dealing with such extraordinary challenges requires serious mental and emotional effort. If you've been through experiences like these—and we all have or will—you know that, while they are painful to face, facing them is the best game in town. Working hard to stay afloat—physically, emotionally, relationally, and financially— is an effort worth making. Frankly, just making the effort to not make things worse counts for a lot, in my opinion. The silver lining is that the experience of dealing with these challenges tends to strengthen us and grow our minds. We wouldn't ask for them or take them on if we didn't have to, but they offer us the opportunity to become stronger, deeper, and more mature characters.

Picture this first kind of work in the reality principle as an old tree on an exposed mountain. Weathered by wind and rain and elements of all kinds, it takes on a unique shape. Its roots and trunk become stronger. We want to be like that tree.

The second level of work in the reality principle builds on the first one, but it is a whole different ball game. It is the work of intentionally taking on difficulties in order to grow. This is a much less common approach to life, but the kind of approach that leads to an even greater sense of meaning and satisfaction. Not only do we take life as it comes to us, we dive in when we don't have to.

Think about people you know—or maybe even yourself—who challenge themselves by their own choices. For example, I have a friend who is not particularly athletic who signed up to run a half-marathon to support cancer research. I'll bet you have a friend like that, too. Then there's the friend who learns to play the piano, speak a new language, or cook. I am always amazed at the hard-core fitness enthusiast who, each year, takes it up another level. The bumper decals say it all: 13.1, 26.2, 70.3, 140.6. It's awe-inspiring to watch someone reach beyond their limits when they don't have to.

Last summer, I went on an organized, moderately challenging hiking trip with a group of a dozen or so forty-something professionals. After four days and thirty-plus miles of hiking, we got to talking about why we would choose to work so hard on a vacation. One of the women said something I thought was really telling: "I sit behind a desk all day, so I want to get out of my comfort zone and do something different. After a trip like this, I smile to myself and say, 'Hey, I'm outdoorsy!'" That is a wonderful example of how taking on work can actually lead to pleasure.

We can push ourselves like this in the psychological realm, too. We can do our best to cope with our emotional lives and we can also take it up a notch to have a richer experience. It's like the difference between staying afloat and swimming, or between surviving and thriving.

When my husband and I were dating, he said something to me that caught my attention. It was an indication that he was that second-level kind of person. He said, "I'm okay being single but I really want to be in a relationship because there's nothing like a relationship to grow you. What I mean is, when I'm in a relationship, I am challenged to grow in ways I can never be when I'm on my own." He had a very different mind-set from other men I had dated before. He was showing me that he had a real interest in growing as a person, in putting himself in situations that would challenge him emotionally. It's one of the main reasons I married him.

Perhaps you are that kind of person, too—the kind of person whose life is working effectively but is troubled by a gnawing sense of dissatisfaction. Perhaps you feel like you are just marking time, lacking a sense of meaning in the rat race life in the modern world can sometimes be. You look at all the accomplishments of your life—all the ways in which you are working in your life pretty well—and you ask yourself, is it enough? Do I want something different? Does my life have meaning? Purpose? Am I at peace?

These are the questions I work with every day in my life and practice as a psychoanalyst. These are the questions that lead us to work at a deeper level. We shift from working on the outside to working on the inside, too. The upward path turns into a downward path, too. We begin to understand what it really means to grow from the inside out. And we embrace the reality that it takes hard work to do it.

CHAPTER FOUR

THERE IS NO SUCH THING AS MAGIC...OR PERFECTION ...OR FOREVER

On Acceptance

BE FOREWARNED. YOU'RE NOT GOING to like this chapter, at least not at first. I'm going to give you a dose of tough love. It's going to be a hard pill to swallow. I'm going to burst a few bubbles, dispel a few myths, and tell it to you like it really is. Remember, I told you this was coming. I only hope that you can forgive me now and maybe—just maybe—you will be able to thank me later.

In his landmark book *The Road Less Traveled*, M. Scott Peck had the courage to say it from the start: "Life is difficult."[9] Psychoanalyst Frieda Fromm-Reichmann conveyed the same truth in the face of protests to her struggling patient: "I never promised you a rose garden."[10] Somewhere along the way, your parents broke the news to you, too: Life isn't fair. And they were all right.

As we mature and turn more and more toward reality, we must face it as it is. We must come to terms with its nature. Life is not always as we wish it would be. We wish we could live without pain, but we can't. We wish we would always get what we want and feel we deserve, but we don't. We wish that our loved ones would never die, but they do. And no matter how hard we wish, how loud we protest, or how well we behave, we can't make these fundamental realities disappear.

This essential truth was the subject of my clinical psychology dissertation, *Who's to Blame When Bad Things Happen to Good People? Causal Attributions for Uncontrollable Negative Events.* The title may sound kind of fancy, but the study wasn't all that complicated. I surveyed about 400 college students and asked them what they thought about the potential causes of some extremely traumatic events such as the Holocaust, earthquakes, and cancer. I was interested in how religious people might differ from nonreligious people in their views about the causes of these kinds of life experiences. You can probably guess that, indeed, they do.

When I talked with my mother about my project, she intuitively understood what I was researching and writing about. My mom had a great sense of humor and, as a way to lend support during that time, she sent me a comic strip from "Hägar the Horrible." In the first frame of the comic strip, Hägar is standing at the bow of his ship, being pummeled by the downpour of a thunder-and-lightning storm. He is looking up to the heavens, hands raised in protest, saying, "Why me?!?" In the second frame, a voice responds from the heavens, saying, "Why not?!?"

Just like Hägar the Horrible, we all need to learn an important lesson about life. Whether we attribute what happens to us in life to the God of the heavens or Mother Nature or just dumb luck, we cannot ignore the voice of reality. As the Psalmist said, "The rain falls on the just and the unjust alike" (Matthew 5:45). Or as your teenage son might say, "Shit happens." My mother understood that if you can simply accept this reality, it might even make you smile.

In this chapter, I want to explore with you how we fight accepting this fundamental reality and how fighting actually *adds* to our suffering. We lose a lot of time and waste a lot of energy when we rage at the tides, protesting a reality that we cannot change rather than doing what we can to deal with life as it is. When we can accept reality as it is, we get the chance to deal with it. And dealing with it is the best game in town.

There are three main misconceptions that we rely on, hoping they will protect us from having to accept reality as it is. Melanie Klein called these ideas *omnipotent fantasies*, and she believed they are universal efforts to avoid facing the scary and painful reality that we are limited creatures. They are psychological tricks we use to support the mistaken belief that we are more in control than we actually are. We all have these fantasies, to some degree. We believe in magic, we believe we can be perfect, and we believe that we will live forever.

Now, you may guffaw that you don't believe in magic. After all, it's the twenty-first century. I don't believe in wizards and witches or magic spells. Maybe I enjoy a little escape into the world of *Harry Potter* or *The Lord of the Rings*, but I know they are fantasy.

> *When we can accept reality as it is, we get the chance to deal with it. And dealing with it is the best game in town.*

I live in a modern, scientific world. I know the difference between Narnia and NASA.

But consider the idea that ancient or medieval belief in magic is still present in our day and age; it's just more subtly woven into our worldview. Try some of these modern-day magical ideas on for size. "If I don't think about it, it doesn't exist." "What you don't know can't hurt you." We each have a kind of genie inside us who crosses her arms, blinks her eyes, nods her head, and—bye, bye!—reality just disappears. This is the psychological magic known as *denial*.

We all use this kind of magical thinking from time to time. We may even need a small dose of denial to stay sane. If we were aware of everything, the mind couldn't process it all. By everything I mean all of the complex realities that are around us, as well as the oftentimes contradictory thoughts, feelings, and impulses that are inside us at any given time. Some of these experiences are too much to bear—too painful, too frightening, too overwhelming. If we were constantly in touch with awareness of all the dangers and longings of life, we would not function very well. We would never get out of bed in the morning. We would never have a baby, travel by plane, or take the plunge by getting married, buying a house, or starting a new business. We would never love anyone. The risk would just be too much.

So the mind has developed an elegant kind of security system, where protective maneuvers like denial can be used to keep us from going crazy and to help us cope with the many demands of internal and external reality. By way of denial, we put unwanted and frightening impulses on the shelf; we shut them away. To use a popular psychological term, we "compartmentalize." We unconsciously place them out of awareness so we can deal. In this limited way, denial is helpful.

While it may be useful to bury our head in the sand for a day or two because we feel overwhelmed, it becomes problematic if we make a lifestyle out of it—that is, when we deny awareness of important things for too long. For a short time, it may be safe to ignore the unopened bills, the twinge of pain in your knee, the rash on the breast, the emotional distance of a loved one, the nagging feeling of guilt, or the weather report about the upcoming storm. Often, such things resolve themselves; no harm, no foul. But when important bits of information about important things grow and persist over time, denial could lead to things getting a whole lot worse.

Take problems with weight, for example. I mean real problems, not just the "I keep losing and gaining the same ten pounds over and over again" weight problem. People who are overweight or obese tend to have serious problems related to denial. It is easy to understand. They turn a blind eye. They tend to not look at themselves in the mirror. They tend to not weigh themselves. They avoid having their photos taken. They don't pay attention to how much food they are eating. These are all subtle but pernicious ways of denying what would otherwise be a very obvious problem. It is the magic of not looking.

We see the same dynamic in physical illness. So often people have a vague awareness that something is wrong with them, but it's too scary to really see it. So they justify the stomach upset or the headache as too much stress. They try to convince themselves that the swelling in their ankles and the dizziness when standing are just the aches and pains of getting older. Or they realize they should go see the doctor but tell themselves that they just don't have the time. By justifying, rationalizing, and putting off facing what they suspect but what they cannot acknowledge, they are casting a kind of spell on themselves. "Abracadabra, what I don't know can't hurt me."

You can probably think of other significant troubles in life that you cope with through the magic of denial. Look the other way and you won't see the obvious signs that your partner is having an affair. Leave the mail unopened and you won't know that your mortgage payment is overdue or your bank account is overdrawn. Don't speak to your loved one about the fight you just had and it will pass. Magical thinking allows us to believe that avoiding and denying these realities will make them go away. However, when we stop to think, it's easy to see how relying on magic makes them worse and how facing them just might make them better.

There's another kind of magic that's also pervasive in the human mind-set. In fact, it is so pervasive that it has probably been a part of the human worldview since the dawn of time. This is the magical belief that good things come to us as rewards and bad things come to us as punishment. I call it magic because it is based on the belief that we can control what happens to us. It refuses to acknowledge the disappointing fact that while we can *influence* what happens to us, we can't *control* it.

For millennia, human beings have believed—or at least wanted to believe—that there is more rhyme and reason to the natural world than there probably is. And up until the relatively recent shift to a more "scientific" worldview, we believed that the gods were behind it all. The idea of gods rewarding good deeds and punishing wrongdoing can be found in many systems, whether you think of Zeus and the Greek pantheon, Yahweh, Allah, Jesus, or most other conceptions of the divine. Prosperity, peace, and health are viewed as rewards. If we have them, we must have pleased the gods. Struggle, failure, strife, and illness are seen as punishments. If bad things only happen to bad people, and we experience them, then we must have done something wrong.

One has only to think of the biblical story of poor Job to see how hard it has been for folks to shake this reward-punishment mentality. The story is about how an apparently righteous man loses everything—his servants, his children, his camels and sheep, his riches, and his health—apparently through no fault of his own. I say "apparently" because his wife and his so-called friends could not believe that his suffering came through no fault of his own. They were too invested in maintaining their belief that life is fair, that you get what you deserve. All they could think about was what Job must have done wrong. As Job protested his innocence, they thought he was the one in denial!

The heart of the story is Job's poignant breakdown and encounter with the God whom he honors and serves. Job never actually curses God, righteous as he is. Rather, Job curses the day that he was born. He does not blame God for his troubles, but he does grieve them. And God meets him there. God speaks to him of ineffable mystery. God shows him that there is a divine logic beyond human understanding. There are exceptions to the general reward-punishment principle that we simply cannot comprehend. Sometimes the righteous suffer. It is a fact of life.

The story of Job is supposed to be a lesson in accepting that life is fundamentally beyond our understanding—that, to put it plainly, sometimes shit just happens and we can't understand why.

This message is wise and true, but there is irony in the story, too. The irony is that this profound insight is couched in the very same worldview it is trying to challenge. While a different kind of rhyme and reason is offered, it rests on the very same reward-punishment principle. It just has a twist.

The story begins with the idea that God and Satan are competing with each other to see how righteous Job really is. Suffering is seen as a test of righteousness. When Job passes this test, his health, riches, and family are restored and then some. In the end, Job is rewarded for being righteous, after all. Job rides off into the sunset, rewarded for being such a good guy. The storyteller has backed himself into the same corner he was trying to get out of! It's hard to resist that Hollywood ending.

It is difficult for us to shake the wish that life should be fair, that we will get what we deserve. We want to understand life's rhyme and reason so we can predict it and therefore imagine we can control it. With effort, we can loosen our grip on this wishful worldview. We can get closer to accepting life on life's terms. The wisest among us can accept that life will always remain a mystery to us, at least to some degree. The humblest among us can get closer to accepting that we ultimately cannot control life, but must take it as it comes and do the best we can.

Even with this wise and humble understanding, we can't help but try to maintain the belief that someone, somewhere is in control. I confess that I do it, too. But I think the belief in someone, somewhere is a matter of faith. And faith is different from magic. Faith takes us to the belief that someone, somewhere understands the sense of things. Magic takes us one step further, to the belief that if we can get in the good graces of that someone, then good will come to us. We don't just believe in someone, we believe we can control that someone. We believe that we can convince him or her to do things our way. That's why I call it magic.

Now, I've got to add insult to injury by letting you know that there's no such thing as perfection, either. No one is perfect. Not you, not me. Not your mama, not your daddy. Not your pastor, not your president, and not even your analyst. I know it's kind of a downer, but still it's true.

In one way, we can understand the pursuit of perfection as another effort at control. If I am perfect, I will succeed. I will never fail. I will never disappoint or be disappointed. I will never hurt anyone or be hurt by anyone. I will never say or do anything wrong. If I am perfectly righteous, good will come to me and bad will stay away. Perfection protects me from the harsh judgment of the gods and puts me in their good graces. I will have found the magic that keeps me safe.

But the pursuit of perfection has another level to it, too. Underneath it all, I think most of us imagine that if we were perfect, we'd be happy. We're looking not only for a safe life but also for a happy one.

How many of us have imagined that if we were prettier, we would be happier? Perhaps for you it would be smarter, stronger, richer, funnier, or thinner. I know that I have shed my share of tears anguishing over what I lack and imagining how much happier I would be if I had it all. It's easy to become concrete and materialistic about these matters, too. We imagine that happiness is somehow connected to driving the right car, throwing the best party, graduating from the most prestigious school, or having the most impressive job. We believe the key to our happiness is to find what we are missing. We wish to be complete.

It takes a lot of hard psychological work to realize that our efforts at having it all are in vain. First of all, no one is perfect, no one has it all. And second, even if we did, it wouldn't get us to where we really want to go. Because happiness is based essentially in love. And love has very little to do with perfection. It is, as they say, a horse of a different color.

This wisdom is conveyed beautifully in the children's story *The Velveteen Rabbit*,[11] a tale that is both simple and profound. It has captured the hearts and minds of generations since it was written by Margery Williams in 1922. If you don't know it, you've got to read it.

The story is about a little boy who is given a stuffed animal for Christmas, the Velveteen Rabbit. While it is a soft and lovely rabbit, it does not have the appeal of the more expensive, mechanical, and fancy toys in the boy's collection. So it is soon forgotten, overshadowed by the more exciting toys in the boy's nursery. The Rabbit, however, makes friends with another long-forgotten toy, the Skin Horse, the shabby veteran of the nursery that had been the favorite toy of the boy's uncle many years before.

As the two stuffed animals are discussing the Rabbit's inferiority complex, the Skin Horse shares some wisdom. A toy becomes real if its owner really loves it.

Williams writes, "'What is REAL?' asked the Rabbit one day, when they were lying side by side near the nursery fender, before Nana came to tidy the room. 'Does it mean having things that buzz inside you and a stick-out handle?' 'Real isn't how you are made,' said the Skin Horse. 'It's a thing that happens to you. When a child loves you for a long, long time, not just to play with, but REALLY loves you, then you become REAL.'"

Oh, I just love this next part. "'Does it hurt?' asked the Rabbit. 'Sometimes,' said the Skin Horse, for he was always truthful. 'When you are Real you don't mind being hurt.' 'Does it happen all at once, like being wound up,' he asked, 'or bit by bit?' 'It doesn't happen all at once,' said the Skin Horse. 'You become. It takes a long time. That's why it doesn't often happen to people who break easily, or have sharp edges, or who have to be carefully kept. Generally, by the time you are Real, most of your hair has been loved off, and your eyes drop out and you get loose in the joints and very shabby. But these things don't matter at all, because once you are Real you can't be ugly, except to people who don't understand.'"

With the help of the wise Skin Horse, we begin to get it. We begin to understand that perfection may be fancy, but it isn't real, and it certainly isn't love. In some ways, perfection doesn't encourage love, either. In fact, it often discourages it. Like the Skin Horse suggests, the easier you break, the sharper your edges, the more you need to be carefully kept, the harder it is to love you. Perfection has a kind of unexpected fragility. It doesn't have the sturdiness needed for the rough-and-tumble of an ordinary, happy, and *real* life.

Just in case you don't know the rest of the story, the Velveteen Rabbit gets his chance to become real. One evening, Nana couldn't find the stuffed dog that always slept with the boy, so she offered the old bunny as a substitute. From that night onward, the Rabbit became the boy's companion in both sleep and play. When the Rabbit was misplaced one day, Nana had to come outside to find him because the boy could not sleep without him. At that moment, the boy announced that the Rabbit had become real.

The Rabbit understood why: He was loved. The secret of this story is that you can't make anyone love you. It just happens. You may be admired because you are fancy or beautiful or polished or deep. But admiration isn't love. It doesn't stand the test of time. It doesn't weather the storms of life. Love is developed through difficult experiences, through scary nights, through the ups and downs of daily life. It happens over time—"bit by bit," as both Margery Williams and Melanie Klein have said. And it comes through suffering. That's what makes it real.

Accepting life on life's terms involves a shift to this more humble attitude. We are who we are. Just human beings. The crown of creation with feet of clay. There is no magic, there is no perfection. And, last but not least, there is no forever.

We human beings fight against the reality that time passes, that loss is inevitable. We find it very difficult to accept that there are forces beyond our control that influence us in the most ultimate of ways. We must be reminded that, in this life of flux and change, there are still two certainties: death and taxes.

There is a story in Greek mythology about a fellow named Orpheus who had an extremely difficult time accepting the realities and limitations of life, including death. Perhaps it was because, though human, he seemed to have magical powers. He was a phenomenal musician. The story goes that his music was so enchanting that he could charm the pants off anything and anyone. Stones came to life at the sound of his voice. Playing his lyre, he could even outsing the Sirens.

Orpheus dared to believe that he could beguile death itself. When his beloved wife Eurydice died on the day of their wedding, Orpheus was overcome with a grief that he could not bear. He was devastated. He sang as he grieved, and then he sang some more. Moved by his songs of despair, the nymphs and the gods suggested Orpheus go to the underworld and try to get Eurydice back from the dead. Now this was no small undertaking. It would mean that he would have to use his music to charm the gods of death themselves. Not known for their sympathy and compassion, the gods Hades and Persephone would be one tough crowd.

So down Orpheus went, deep into the underworld. Down he went, refusing to accept the fact of his wife's mortality. But even more than that, he made that descent because he could not accept his own mortality. He could not accept the fact that he was limited in what he could do. Talented musician that he was, as deep as his love for his wife was, he was still a mere mortal.

The story eggs us on. We, too, want to believe that Orpheus could bring his beloved back to life. We admire such love. We idealize it. We cheer for Orpheus in our hearts. And so did Hades and Persephone. The hardest hearts the world can imagine— Mr. and Mrs. Death themselves—were softened by the velvety voice of the crooner and captured by the melody of his lyre. They granted him permission to take Eurydice back to the land of the living. There was only one condition. She must follow behind him in the upward journey and he could not look back until they both set foot on terra firma.

Orpheus was thrilled, delighted to be given a second chance with his beloved Eurydice. So they began the arduous journey upward. But soon enough, Orpheus, in his love for his wife—in his genuine human love and concern—became anxious. He wanted to keep an eye on his Eurydice. He wanted to look back to make sure she was all right. He wanted to check to make sure she was still there. But he reminded himself that he couldn't look back without losing her forever. So he kept going, upward and then upward some more. Yet he couldn't shake his concern. He worried that perhaps she had been wounded. Perhaps she had fallen behind. He could not stand not knowing. The closer he got to the threshold of life, the more excited he got—and the more desperate, too.

You may know the end of the story. As soon as he set foot in the land of the living, he looked back. Eurydice was there, one step away from cheating death. But Orpheus looked too soon. And so she vanished. Now not even Orpheus could sing her back to life. She was gone forever.

This poignant story is often interpreted as a tragedy, a failure on Orpheus's part. He is judged as lacking true love, trust, and faith. Even worse, he is judged for being impatient, selfish, and even arrogant. I think we interpret the story in these ways because we all want to keep believing that a perfect love could overcome death. If only Orpheus had that love, he could have done it. He could have brought her back. Or so we want to believe.

I want to suggest an alternative interpretation. Perhaps the story of Orpheus and Eurydice is actually a story about accepting reality. Death, loss, and limitations are inevitable in life. They are at the heart of being human. Even for the most talented, the most charming, or the most loving among us, there is no way around it. We are all mere mortals. We may be able to cleverly get around taxes, but not death.

Ironically, part of being human is that we don't want to accept the fact that we are human. Like Orpheus, we have this enduring belief that we are more powerful than we are. In Orpheus's story, it is writ large. We believe that we have power over the gods, which is another way of saying that we have power over death.

The real tragedy of this story is that Orpheus was so intent on doing what he could *not* do that he was unable to do what he *could* do. Orpheus's true limitation was not an inability to overcome death through perfect love. It was his inability to grieve and move on.

One of the sources of unhappiness in life is our denial of the passage of time. We live our lives as if we have forever. We put off until tomorrow what we can do today. In so doing, the present moment slips away. We miss the chance to be here now. That is the real loss. And, at some level, we know it. We are plagued by the vague awareness that our lives are just passing us by. We worry that we will not appreciate what we actually have until it is too late—until it is gone.

Bronnie Ware, an Australian nurse who spent many years providing palliative care to the dying, wrote a blog and then a book about this stunning psychological reality. *The Top Five Regrets of the Dying*[12] catalogs the suffering that comes when we cannot accept that time stops for no one. These are the profound regrets that her patients expressed to her:

1. I wish I'd had the courage to live a life true to myself, not the life others expected of me.
2. I wish I hadn't worked so hard.
3. I wish I'd had the courage to express my feelings.
4. I wish I had stayed in touch with my friends.
5. I wish that I had let myself be happier.

These pointed observations are in the spirit of the wisdom I am trying to convey. When we live under the spell of magic, when we allow ourselves to be held captive by the pursuit of perfection, and when we ignore the preciousness of each moment, we lose perspective about what really matters. Ware's observations point to the deepest longings of the human heart. We long to be true to ourselves. We long to enjoy the life we have while we have it. We long to experience the love that is right in front of us.

If we can accept life on life's terms, we get to engage with it in a real way. This is such a gift. Rather than fighting against life, we get to take it in. We get to be nourished by it. We get to have something real that lasts.

Even more, if we can take the good with the bad as it comes to us in life, then there is less need to look back with regret. There is less need to turn back to try to recapture what has been lost. We are able to grieve what has been lost on the outside because it already has a lasting home in our hearts.

⌒

Among the many lessons about life taught by the Buddha, two stand out to me. One is that life is suffering. The other is that the key to happiness is to love the life you have.

It is necessary to accept that there is suffering in life. But if we can suffer this first disillusionment, we are able to mitigate some of the unnecessary sufferings that might otherwise follow. Unnecessary suffering comes from maintaining unrealistic expectations of ourselves and others. When we keep insisting that we should have more than we have or be more than we are, we live in a constant state of disappointment. When we can engage the life we do have— limited as it is—we actually have the chance to develop and even enjoy it. In other words, accepting life is the gateway to loving it.

It is difficult to digest this essential truth. As I stated early on, accepting life on life's terms can be a hard pill to swallow. You may be thinking that what I'm *really* saying is that we just have to accept that life is a big fat disappointment. It might even sound like I am saying that the best we can do is settle for mediocrity and be depressed about it. Is there really no point in trying to improve, or fight for more, or reach beyond what we know? Am I saying that dreamers shouldn't dream, inventors shouldn't invent, and explorers shouldn't explore? These notions couldn't be further from the truth.

What I am saying is that there is freedom in taking life as it comes to us—the good with the bad, the wonderful with the tragic, the love with the loss, and the life with the death. When we embrace it all, then we have a real chance to enjoy life, to value our experiences, and to mine the treasures that are there for the taking.

> *Freedom is found in accepting our limitations rather than fighting them. Acceptance is the doorway to our real strength and potential.*

Freedom is found in accepting our limitations rather than fighting them. Acceptance is the doorway to our real strength and potential. I promise to talk more about this in the upcoming chapters. I want to show you how, when we surrender to the reality of who we are, we give ourselves a chance to do what we can do.

Freedom within limits is the powerful message of Reinhold Niebuhr's classic prayer, so essential to the work of the Twelve Steps: "God, grant me the serenity to accept the things I cannot change, the courage to change the things I can change, and the wisdom to know the difference."[13] As I see it, a life guided by the principles of this prayer promises to be a pretty satisfying one.

CHAPTER FIVE

SLOW AND STEADY WINS THE RACE

On Humility

AFTER THAT LAST CHAPTER I hope you've taken a break. Maybe you took a walk around the block, had a cup of coffee, or sat in quiet reflection. It's a lot to take in. I wouldn't blame you if you needed to sleep on it or even put it aside for a while. Accepting life on life's terms isn't easy. But it is the foundation upon which we can build a satisfying, meaningful, and—dare I say—happy life.

So in this chapter, I'm going to build upon this foundation by sharing a secret with you. I'm going to start with a few cautionary words and then I'm going to lay out for you a way of approaching life that promises to lead to this satisfying, meaningful, and even happy way of being. And it is a way that works.

First, a few words to the wise.

Once we surrender to accepting reality as it is, we tend to cope with life in a rather predictable but problematic way. Once we bite the bullet, we puff ourselves up by saying, "No need to worry. Reality doesn't really bother me. I can take it." Once we decide we're going to get in the game of life-as-it-is, we stand up to our full height, head held high, and say, "I'm not afraid. Bring it on!"

You might wonder why I suggest that this approach to life on life's terms is problematic. I mean, really, it sounds kind of good, doesn't it? If we want to make something of our lives, we need to turn toward life's challenges, screw up our courage, and face them. Right? You might even say that we need this kind of chutzpah to be successful in life—and I would agree. Such an approach only becomes problematic when we take it too far. When, in the process of engaging life, we exaggerate our strengths and ignore our limitations, we become vulnerable to turning a really good approach into a really self-defeating one.

This all-too-human dynamic reminds me of a hilarious scene from the film *Monty Python and the Holy Grail*. The scene has become something of a cult classic. Perhaps you remember King Arthur searching the land for worthy men to join him as Knights of the Round Table. He meets the Black Knight in the woods and invites him to join them in their noble quest. The Black Knight, feeling rather superior, refuses Arthur's offer and tries to prevent him from passing through the woods. They begin a sword fight and Arthur dominates, cutting off the Black Knight's arm. In the face of such a catastrophic injury, the Black Knight remains undaunted. "A mere scratch," he says as he shrugs his shoulder, now gushing blood. Arthur responds incredulously, "Your arm's off!" The Black Knight replies nonchalantly, "I've had worse," goading Arthur to fight some more.

As the fight goes on, Arthur cuts the Black Knight's *other* arm off. But even with blood now gushing out of both shoulders, the Black Knight won't give up. "Just a flesh wound!" Armless, he kicks

Arthur. We are rolling on the floor, laughing at such a ludicrous scene. "I'm invincible!" says the hopelessly cocky Black Knight. By the end of the encounter, the Black Knight has no arms *or* legs, and yet he mocks Arthur as he passes by in victory, "Oh, I see, running away! Come back and take what's coming to you." He has taken Winston Churchill's "never, never give up" way too far.

The Black Knight is a startling example of an aspect of the human psyche that is surprisingly common. Even in the face of insurmountable obstacles, we contemptuously mock reality by saying, "I can do anything. No one can stop me. You can't hurt me, defeat me, or discourage me. I am invincible!" Melanie Klein explored these tactics we so often use in our lives, calling them the *manic defenses*. Beliefs in our self-sufficiency, grandiosity, and triumph protect us from awareness of our limitations and, most especially, from awareness of our need for others.

Now, you might be thinking that such a style is too outrageous to be real, the stuff of silly comedies and not the stuff of real life. But the truth is, this style is so pervasive in human experience that there are probably a thousand examples of it in the wisdom tradition, as well as in the lore of our own day and age. Once you get the hang of it, you will start to see it everywhere. This manic approach to life is as central to human psychological functioning as the lungs are to human physical functioning. To illustrate, let's go back to the Ancient Greeks.

There's no better example of the good-approach-gone-bad than the myth of Daedalus and his son, Icarus. Daedalus was the kind of guy who lived life full throttle but had the good sense to do so safely. He was an amazing craftsman, sculptor, and inventor, credited for inventing the axe, the awl, the bevel, and sails for ships, among many other things. But his most infamous creation was the Labyrinth in Crete, designed at the command of the corrupt King Minos to house the ferocious Minotaur.

According to the legend, King Minos would periodically demand seven girls and seven boys from nearby Athens as payment for the city's recent offenses against him. King Minos would then send the Athenian children into the Labyrinth to be eaten by the Minotaur. Daedalus, who opposed this awful practice, is said to have helped the good Prince Theseus of Athens navigate his mysterious Labyrinth, killing the Minotaur and escaping with the other children.

When King Minos learned that the Minotaur had been killed and the children had been saved, he was rightly convinced that Daedalus had been behind it. As a result, King Minos imprisoned Daedalus and his son Icarus. Now Daedalus was no dummy, so he began to think about how he and Icarus could bust out of the joint. Escape by water or land would just be too obvious and therefore too dangerous. King Minos and his men would have eyes everywhere. Daedalus needed an idea with the element of surprise. Creative inventor that he was, he looked up to the sky and hatched a plan. No one would imagine an escape through the air, he thought. Perhaps they could fly like the birds. So Daedalus made two pairs of wings from feathers and wax. Ingenuity at its best.

Before they took flight, Daedalus had a long talk with his son, Icarus. Though Daedalus was brilliant and creative, he also was cautious and humble. He warned Icarus to be careful, for the wings were fragile and vulnerable to the elements. If they flew too high, the sun might melt the wax and the wings would fall apart. Icarus, excited about their adventure, said he understood the need to be careful and was ready to go. So they strapped on their wings, pumped their arms, and—lo and behold!—they began to fly. Up and up they soared. Out and over the sea, they traveled away from Crete toward freedom.

But Icarus got ahead of himself and neglected his father's wise words. He got too excited, overcome by the superhuman thrill of being able to fly. He took his flight too far, too close to the sun. As his father had predicted, the wax began to melt and the wings fell apart. Icarus lost sight of his limitations and gave in to his grandiosity, falling to his death at the bottom of the sea. Sadly, he is remembered not for his courage but for his hubris. As they say, "Pride goeth before a fall."

This myth has stood the test of time because it showcases a problematic approach to life to which we can easily fall prey. We do well to keep Icarus in mind, because we too are prone to ignoring our limitations and taking things too far. We get a thrill out of seeing ourselves as grand, fancy, and able to soar above it all. His is the ultimate cautionary tale.

But rarely do we think much more about his father, Daedalus, although his character reveals a deeper wisdom still. Like Icarus, Daedalus reached for the stars. He was a master of the seemingly impossible. He was an inventor par excellence. Indeed, he was the one who figured out how to fly. Yet his story did not end in disaster; it ended in freedom. What made the difference?

If we contrast Daedalus and Icarus, we discover a subtle but invaluable truth. There is a big difference between healthy ambition and reckless mania. Healthy ambition motivates us to reach beyond ourselves in a constructive way. A bit of mania—in the Kleinian sense—is an aspect of ambition. It is the wellspring of creativity and innovation. In fact, we need a bit of mania in order to grow. It nudges us to pursue our dreams. But it needs to be safeguarded. When tempered by humility, mania can solve riddles and free captives. When unbridled, it can lead to disaster.

Think of this healthy dose of mania when it comes to children. A bit of mania in an overexcited, grandiose sort of way is a normal and essential part of growing up. Without it, we would stay stagnant. With it, we are propelled to reach forward and take the next step in our development. How often does a parent try to help a child with a task that is beyond him or her—whether it is using a spoon, tying shoelaces, or reaching up to the kitchen counter— only to be met with "I can do it myself!" This is a good thing. Even when a child fails, we know there's great value in simply trying. If he can weather the failures and keep at it, one day he will succeed. This is ambition in the best sense of the word.

The trouble comes when we take it too far. In our efforts to embrace our so-called "true potential," we may unwisely take an overly manic approach to life. This is especially true in modern American culture. We relish the idea of being "all that we can be"— and then some. We foster such an attitude in our children. Some therapists encourage it in their clients. Self-help books, New Age philosophy, and motivational speakers tell us that our problem is not that we reach too far but that we do not reach far enough.

So the message that I am conveying may be somewhat surprising, even off-putting to you. It is counterintuitive in the sense that the pursuit of greatness is often considered a healthy aspiration, the essence of the American dream. So if you are feeling skeptical, I get it. Who wants to hear that his or her pursuit of greatness could be a problem? Who wants that bubble to be burst?

It reminds me of the words of legendary feminist Gloria Steinem: "The truth will set you free, but first it will piss you off."

The plain truth is that there is a dark underbelly to the reach-beyond-your-limits approach to life. We don't want to admit it, but it's true. Sometimes our surge toward greatness can be deadly. Even when it doesn't have a tragic end, it often just doesn't work. It can backfire. It can prevent us from getting help when we really need it. It can put us in danger that could have been avoided.

Icarus should have listened to his father, because his father really knew more than he did about a matter of great serious-ness. Cautionary advice may be frustrating because it bursts our manic bubble, but it also can save our life. In small doses, daring to be great leads to success and innovation. That is one part of the story. But in large doses, it can lead to a mighty long fall. We need to heed that part of the story, too.

> *The plain truth is that there is a dark underbelly to the reach-beyond-your-limits approach to life.*

Let me remind you now of another wise tale with which you are likely familiar. Whether you are a student of the ancient classics or modern Disney, you have likely been exposed to the wisdom of one of the greatest storytellers of all time. Fast-forward a thousand years or so beyond the myth of Daedalus and Icarus, and we find our way to Aesop and his fables. Here is a story that is both a cautionary tale and a road map for success.

Once upon a time there were two friends, a tortoise and a hare. The tortoise was a decent fellow, hardworking though a bit boring. The hare was a lively one, as happy as Tigger and as bouncy, too! The hare was a braggart and loved to show off his speed, zipping from here to there, saying, "Look at me! Look at me! No one is faster than me!" The hare also had a tendency to put others down—not an especially flattering quality. In fact, he incessantly teased his friend, the tortoise, for being so slow. The tortoise was very patient and he liked his friend but, one day, he announced that he had had enough.

"You are one annoying rabbit!" the tortoise cried out in frustration. "Yes, you're quick. But you aren't that swift in other ways, if you get my meaning!"

"I have no idea what you're talking about," the hare demurred. "I am swift in every way. No one can beat me!"

"I beg to differ, my friend," said the tortoise. "Even I, slow as I am, can beat you to the finish line."

The gauntlet thrown down, the race was on. They planned a course, arranged the details, and set the start time at dawn the next day.

The tortoise got a good night's sleep so that he could be rested for the race. Unconcerned, the hare partied late into the night, showing up just in time for the race to begin. "No matter," the hare said to himself as he let out a big yawn. "This tortoise is so slow, I could take a nap and still beat him." As he watched the tortoise get off to an even slower start than he could have imagined, the hare decided that a nap actually sounded like a pretty good idea. "Have at it, my dear friend," the hare cajoled. "I'll just have a snooze on this nice rock over here and catch up with you later."

After a while, the hare woke up from his nap, suddenly anxious that perhaps he had gone a bit too far in his nonchalance. But to his great relief, the tortoise hadn't even moved half the distance yet. He still had lots of time.

So the hare cleared the sleepy dust from his eyes and, seeing the tortoise had barely moved an inch farther, decided that he might have even more time than he thought. "A little breakfast sounds good," he said to himself. So he raided the neighbor's garden and had a nice big meal of carrots and cabbage, which made him sleepy again. He glanced at the tortoise—who had made some good progress by now. "No worries," the hare thought to himself. "It will be even more fun to beat the poor sap after I've had yet another nap!" Lying down under the hot sun with a full belly, the hare enjoyed another forty winks.

The hare happily dreamt of the look of humiliation on the tortoise's face when he zipped past him to victory. But as he continued to snooze, he began to have a vague sense that the day was getting cooler, the sky a bit darker. He woke with a start, looked around, and could not see the tortoise anywhere. So the hare sprang into action and ran as fast as he could along the race course. Soon enough, he could see the tortoise plodding ahead, just a few steps from the finish line. *I can do this,* the hare thought to himself. *I'm fast as lightning!* But despite his great speed and burst of determination, the hare was one step shy of beating the tortoise to the finish line. Out of breath, he collapsed in a heap of disgrace.

The hare looked over at the tortoise, ready to be heckled by the winner. Smiling, the tortoise said simply, "Slow and steady wins the race . . . every time."

It's not difficult to relate to the character of the hare in Aesop's famous fable. I know that I can. As the youngest child in my family, I know what it is like to want to feel quicker, smarter, and more clever than I really am. Ashamed, I also must admit that I know what it feels like to want to feel superior, to look down on others and see them as smaller, slower, and dimmer. It's not an attractive look, I know. But it is very human.

Ever since I can remember, I was the kind of kid who had big dreams. No doubt about it, I had a good dose of hare in my personality. I wanted to cross the finish line first *and* make it look easy! For many of my junior high school years, I used to fantasize about being a famous preacher or jazz musician. I would hang out alone in my room for hours, pretending that I was delivering a big speech or playing an awesome solo to the applause of the crowds. I liked the idea of being famous, fancy, and important. I wanted to be in the limelight.

Lucky for me, I had a fair dose of tortoise in my personality, too. I really can't take much credit for this disposition, temperament being the inheritance that it is. But I intuitively understood the value of hard work and didn't shy away from it. I was the kid who practiced for hours and hours, whether it was shooting hoops in the driveway, practicing scales on my trumpet, or hitting the homework as soon as I came home from school. I was determined to get things just right. I was a perfectionist—and I still am. I took pride in my work, and that helped me to develop and grow, but often under the unnecessary pressure of believing I could be—and should be—bigger than I was.

My father loves to tell the story of how I went about learning to ride a bicycle. I started out on my Sears Roebuck two-wheeler with the requisite training wheels. We lived on a pretty quiet street, so I could ride up and down the block and practice my balance. Soon the day came when my dad took the training wheels off. I was nervous, of course. I hated failure almost more than I loved success. So I was careful, a bit wobbly at first. But once I got going, I was like the hare—thrilled, proud of myself, and, well, a bit cocky. Of course, it was inevitable that I would lose my balance and fall over. Down I went, feeling awful and totally humiliated. So what did I do next? I looked at my father through teary eyes and kicked the bicycle!

As my friend from Texas would say, I was trying to be big, but little got me.

It is such a human tendency to puff ourselves up in an effort to get some distance from the painful awareness that we are small and vulnerable, less capable than we wish to be. It is a kind of protection—a bit of the old magic, if you will—that helps us feel better in the short

Cultivating a sympathetic attitude toward our smallness is a key to emotional health.

term but much worse in the long term. When we try to make ourselves bigger than we really are, we fall from an even greater height. Failure then feels all the more humiliating. Like the Emperor parading down Main Street wearing no clothes, we feel that we have been revealed for who we truly are—not just a kid learning to ride a bicycle, but a fraud.

Cultivating a sympathetic attitude toward our smallness is a key to emotional health. When we can view our inadequacies, innocence, and vulnerabilities with kindness and compassion, we are able to learn through failure without that sense of humiliation. Then falling off the bicycle is just falling off the bicycle. We dust ourselves off, get back on, and try again. But when we shun our smallness, the process of learning and growing is much more painful than it needs to be. Falling off the bicycle becomes an accusation of our incompetence rather than an opportunity to learn. Such a harsh attitude discourages rather than encourages the effort to put ourselves in a more humble position that allows for real growth.

Perhaps you can see how this too-big-for-your-britches approach to life undermines the goal we wish to attain. By being in a hurry to grow up—like the hare—we actually thwart our own success in growing up. We get ahead of ourselves. We make more mistakes. We cut corners and pay for them later. We may learn the easy way, but not necessarily the best way. The old adage puts it like this: The slower you go, the sooner you get there. Slow, disciplined, incremental growth, like the tortoise, is the kind of approach that leads to lasting change.

There is another unfortunate downside of this self-sufficient, grandiose, and hurried approach to life. Not only do we go about life with a backfiring strategy, but we also go it alone. We don't allow ourselves to make good use of help from others that is available to us. We often don't realize just how counterproductive a strategy this is. We often have it backward. While our aim is to get bigger, we wind up making ourselves smaller, cut off from the help we need in order to learn, grow, and improve.

It is an inescapable reality that human beings need each other in order to grow. We are a fundamentally interdependent species. Don't let all that Wild West–style bravado fool you. We may like to think that we are a self-sufficient, pull-yourselves-up-by-your-bootstraps kind of people. We go about our lives with the philosophy of "don't let them see you cry or sweat or hesitate or fail," and we think that is a good thing. We cringe at the thought of being called a "girlie man" or a "crybaby." Yet, underneath it all, we know that we really do need a helping hand.

The only way we can really grow—the only way to get big in the proper sense—is by learning from those who know more than we do and receiving training from those who are more capable than we are. Growth is an interactive endeavor. We need parents, brothers and sisters, friends, teachers, and mentors of all kinds to help us. It really does take a village.

Oddly enough, in our modern American middle-class society, mothers seem to be the ones who most get lost in this frantic effort to do everything alone. This is particularly true for working moms. As the commercial says, she prides herself on being able to bring home the bacon, fry it up in a pan, and never let her husband forget he's a man. As the modern-day superhero, the working mom tries to be all things to all people. Even though she is tired and could use some support, she puts on her cape every day and tries to save the world.

No wonder we have been called the Prozac generation! We make things too hard on ourselves. And, to make matters worse, we feel pressure to do it all with a smile on our face. If only we could make the shift from self-sufficiency to interdependency. If only we could let a brother help a sister out.

There is a model of interdependency made famous by the Toyota Motor Corporation that reflects this psychoanalytic wisdom. *Kaizen* is the Japanese philosophy of long-term growth and continuous improvement that involves the whole community rather than just one person at the top. Consistent with the psychoanalytic principles described herein, *kaizen* endorses the value of incremental change over sudden, radical transformation. The method promotes the practice of paying attention to the small details, looking for ways to improve on an ongoing basis, and taking input from individuals at every level of the organization, no matter how big or small.

The philosophy of *kaizen* is a kind of safeguard for the manic approach to organizational life that is particularly common in the West, in the sense that it is opposed to self-sufficiency, grandiosity, and fierce competitiveness. It views progress as the result of teamwork, interdependency, and group efficiency as opposed to flashes of brilliance, individual achievement, or sudden innovation. "You're on your own" is replaced with "We're all in this together." "I'm the king of the hill" is transformed into "One small step can change your life."

The beauty of the *kaizen* approach is that it also is reliable in the face of failure. The folks at Toyota Motor Corporation know this very well. In the face of its failure to maintain quality control regarding safety, Toyota learned that the *kaizen* way facilitates openness to feedback of all kinds, including feedback that one has failed to be open to feedback. The philosophy understands that failure is part of life, appreciating that limitations and mistakes are inevitable in the complex functioning of any organization. In that mind-set, there is always a method in place to respond to failures in the spirit of continuous improvement.

Another model for the *kaizen* way can be found in the Catholic monastic tradition of St. Benedict. Back in the fifth century,

St. Benedict established his monastic community by encouraging his monks to build their lives on three individual and community principles. To join the community, each monk took vows of stability, obedience, and *conversatio morum*. Stability is the commitment to one place, one people, and one vocation for a lifetime. Obedience is the commitment to submission to authority within that community, a practice that may sound restricting but is essentially about knowing one's place in the best sense. Alongside the pillars of these two vows is the third, the commitment to *conversatio morum*, loosely translated as "continual conversion." The spirit of the monk's life is to be one of endless learning, refining, and discovery in the context of a supportive community. He renews his vows every day. He lives his life in psychoanalyst Wilfred Bion's spirit of learning through experience.

There is profound wisdom from the desert fathers of St. Benedict's time. When asked the question "What do you monks do in there all day?" they answered, "We fall and get up, fall and get up again."

The more we can become comfortable with being small, needing help, and depending on others who know more than we do and are more capable than we are, the more we are open to receiving the help they have to give. The more comfortable we can be with our "baby selves," the more we can sustain being in the position of learner. Simply put, this is the position of humility.

If we want to learn, we must take the path of humility. Surprisingly, it is not the place where we begin. Like the capacity to work, humility is a psychological achievement. It requires the disciplined effort to see ourselves as we really are—neither bigger than we are nor smaller than we are. When we begin there, we have the opportunity to move forward in a new and more effective way.

When I was in college, struggling with my wish to be big and fancy yet becoming aware of its pitfalls, I came across a poem—really, a prayer—that made a lasting impression on me. It's from a little book of Christian poetry by Ruth Harms Calkin.[14] It goes like this:

> You know, Lord, how I serve You
> With great emotional fervor
> In the limelight.
>
> You know how eagerly I speak for You
> At a women's club.
> You know how I effervesce when I promote
> A fellowship group.
>
> You know my genuine enthusiasm
> At a Bible study.
>
> But how would I react, I wonder . . .
> If You pointed me to a basin of water
> And asked me to wash the calloused feet
> Of a bent and wrinkled old woman
>
> Day after day
> Month after month
> In a room where nobody saw
> And nobody knew.

In a way I loved this poem, and in a way I hated it. I sensed that it had a message that I needed to hear. I knew it was a discipline that I needed to develop.

It's funny to me how this poem has stuck with me all these years. I was probably about twenty years old when I first read it. At that time, I saw myself on a path to being an effervescent, enthusiastic leader in the limelight. But I was also insecure inside. Thanks to a lot of help from wise parents, therapists, and teachers, I came to see that I neurotically needed the applause to reassure myself that I was good enough. Slowly, over time, as I began to feel more comfortable in my own skin, I found that I needed the applause less and less. Then I began to see the appeal of this quiet, behind-the-scenes place where I could discover a different kind of satisfaction and meaning.

The work of being a psychoanalyst is a lot like the work that Ruth Harms Calkin describes at the end of her poem. Day after day, month after month, in a room known for its privacy and confidentiality, I quietly meet with another person. Whether it is an old woman or a young man, bent and wrinkled or high-strung and anxious, they come. There is no applause, no real audience to speak of. There is just the two of us, engaged in an intimate exchange with no witnesses. The work of tending the mind, heart, and soul of another turns out to be a lot like the humble act of washing someone's feet.

I am most grateful for the discovery that quiet, humble work can build a solid foundation from which real creativity and success can stem. I suppose this is not the only way, but it has become the way for me. When I rein in my impulses to live in a flashy, fancy, conspicuous way, I find myself more rested, more centered, and more grounded. It is the only way I know to keep at the daily discipline of being a psychoanalyst. It is simple, quiet work that yields meaningful rewards.

Success in so many aspects of life, especially creative endeavors, rests on this simple foundation, too. Innovation of all kinds is rooted in the basics. You've got to work the fundamentals. You've got to keep practicing your scales. It takes simple, private, humble, even mundane daily effort. No one will ever know all the work you invested to make what you do look so easy.

I spend a lot of time in the workshop that is my therapy office. I have tried to create a space that is simple and not too fancy. It looks a lot like a living room with a desk in the corner, warm and relaxed, neat and inviting. I selected art with the wisdom of psychoanalysis in mind. As a reminder that life is a journey, I chose images of doors, paths, and winding roads. A few years after I first set up my office, I added a special piece to mark my achievement in completing psychoanalytic training. It is a metalwork design of the Tree of Life, made by poor workers in Haiti who pounded into shape the metal from recycled oil barrels. To me, the work of psychoanalysis is like making something beautiful out of the scraps that lie within our reach.

Over my desk hangs a black-and-white photograph of a water pitcher and basin next to a neatly stacked set of white towels. I selected it years ago because I liked how the image conveyed for me the work of service, the cleansing of the soul, and the new beginning symbolized by washing. One day while I was working with a patient, I glanced over at the photograph and made the connection for the first time. Here I was, decades later, doing the work of Ruth Harms Calkin's poem. I was washing the callused feet of a bent and wrinkled old woman, in a room where nobody saw and nobody knew.

That moment of insight brought a sense of satisfaction, as I realized that I was making progress along my journey, too. Each day, I work toward becoming more of who I am. Not bigger, not smaller. Just me. That is the wisdom of humility that I try to foster in my own life and the wisdom I hope to pass along.

~

CHAPTER SIX

LIFE IS NOT AN ENTITLEMENT; IT IS A GIFT

On Gratitude

GRATITUDE IS THE LINCHPIN OF a satisfying life. It is the attitude that holds life's complexities together in a constructive way. It helps us sort through life's ambiguities, contradictions, and sufferings to discover the threads of goodness woven through them. The essential nature of gratitude is to focus on the good that is present in one's life and to appreciate it as a gift to be cherished. A grateful attitude stands in contrast to our unfortunate tendency to poison whatever goodness we might have by bitterly focusing on the bad or on the good that is missing. When instead we are guided by the attitude of gratitude, we receive life as a gift that generates feelings of safety, security, and love from and for the giver of the gift. As I will show you, this attitude is an antidote to many psychological troubles in life.

Take this story as an illustration. A young girl received a pony for her birthday. To this wonderful gift, she responded, "Oh, dear! Who's going to clean up the shit?" Another young girl received a pile of shit for her birthday. To this dubious gift, she responded, "Oh my! Where's the pony?"

Our attitude toward the gifts we receive changes the meaning we make of them. The above story makes this insight plain. On one extreme, we have the girl who receives what most of us would consider a good gift, only to dismiss its goodness and quickly look for, detect, and imagine the bad that is waiting in the wings. At the other end of the continuum, we have the girl who receives what most would consider to be a bad gift, and instinctively overlooks the bad in search of the good that is expected to be there, too.

It would be naïve to expect that we would always look for the good even in the worst of situations. But it would also be tragic if we persisted in turning a good situation into something bad. Hopefully, we are able to find middle ground.

Recognizing the good and receiving it with gratitude is a recipe for emotional health and well-being. This attitude enlarges the possibility that we can make use of the good we have been given and even use it to cope with the difficulties that we have inevitably inherited. What's more, if we can receive the good as a gift—rather than something to which we are entitled—then the humility of the last chapter pairs up with the gratitude of this chapter. And that is a truly winning combination.

⌣

If you look at the teachings of all the great wisdom traditions, you will find many lessons on the fundamental importance of gratitude—such as in the sayings of the Buddha, the teachings of the Talmud and the investigations of the Midrash, the stories of tribes from all around the globe, and, of course, the theories of Melanie Klein.

Let me give you a few examples from my own spiritual tradition, found in the parables of Jesus. The first example is perhaps the most famous. It is the story of a man who had two sons. The younger boy developed quite the reputation; for centuries now, he has been known infamously as the Prodigal Son (Luke 15:11–32).

As the story goes, Junior was not too happy with his family situation, living at home and working for his father. He was impatient and wanted a change. He wanted to see the world. So he said to his father, "Dad, this place blows. I want to go out on my own. I shouldn't have to wait until you die to get my inheritance. I want it now."

The father thought about his son's request, shrugged his shoulders, and said, "Okay. It's up to you. If you want your inheritance now, so be it." So the father divided his estate and gave the son his portion.

If you look at the teachings of all the great wisdom traditions, you will find many lessons on the fundamental importance of gratitude . . .

It didn't take Junior long to get his gear together and hop the next donkey out of town. He traveled to a distant country, blew all of his dough by indulging his every desire, and wound up with nothing left but the shirt on his back. Just when he thought his life couldn't get worse, everything around him fell apart, too. A famine came through the land, so there was no food and very little work. The best he could do was to weasel his way into his neighbor's good graces and earn his keep feeding his neighbor's pigs. The boy was even tempted to eat some of the swine's food himself, just to keep from starving. He thought, *I can't seem to catch a break. What's a rich man's son to do?*

Hungry, dirty, and desperate, the boy came up with an idea. He said to himself, "How many of my father's hired hands have three square meals a day and a clean place to sleep, while I am starving to death? I will swallow my pride and go back home, admit my sin, and beg for a chance to be taken in as one of my father's servants. Dad may be mad at me for all that I've done, but he's a decent guy. He might show me a little mercy."

So he set off on foot, back to his father's home. When he was still a good distance away, he could already see that his father had spotted him and was running down the road toward him. Was his father happy to see him? Or angry? Ready to embrace him? Or hurrying to lock the gate? He didn't know what to expect.

Much to his surprise, his father barreled right into him and gave him a big hug. The son tried to gather up his courage to give his speech but, before he could get two words out, the father was calling the servants to welcome his younger son home. "Look who has finally returned to me! Get him a change of clothes and some new sandals—and put a ring on his finger. We're celebrating. Stoke the fire. Kill the fatted calf. We're going to have a party!"

Happy ending as that might have been, the story didn't end there. The older brother had a part to play in it, too. He was off in the field, doing what he did best—being responsible, hardworking, and respectful to his father. When he came back to the house after the long day's work, he heard all the commotion, the music, and the dancing. "What's happening?" he asked one of the servants.

"Your brother has come and your father is beside himself with joy. He is so happy that Junior is home safe that he is throwing a big party to celebrate."

But the older son wasn't nearly as happy as his father. In fact, he was pretty angry. So he stayed in the kitchen, sulking. Soon, his father came looking for him to see what was wrong. The older son said to his father, "All this time I have been serving you. I have been the model of a good son, taking care of you and looking after your estate. Not once did you throw a party for me—or even give me a young goat so that I could have a barbecue with my friends. But as soon as Junior rolls back in from his trip to Sin City, you kill the fatted calf and invite everyone in town to celebrate. It's just not right. It's just not fair."

The father thought about it, for he knew his son was a serious young man. Taking a deep breath, he sighed. "Son, you are right. You have been by my side all these years, faithful in every way. All that I have is yours. But that being said, it is also right that we have a party for your little brother. After all, he was dead and now he is alive. He was lost and now he is found."

The Parable of the Prodigal Son is quite a story, I know. It really makes you think. It has been interpreted in many different ways, richly layered with meaning as it is. For now, I want to draw out a few elements to help in our search for the keys to a satisfying life. The story is essentially about our relationship with our parents and their relationship with us. Like it or not, the nature of our relationship with our parents—both on the inside and on the outside—is at the heart of how we fare in this wild and precious life.

Like the younger son, we have a deep, often unconscious, attitude toward our parents that thwarts our success in life. We feel entitled. I know, *entitled* is an ugly word, but it describes this attitude so well. At some level, we all struggle with an inner spoiled brat who believes that we deserve to have it all—what we want, when we want it, the way we want it. We don't believe that we should have to wait, to do without, to give back, or to be responsible with what we've been given. And we certainly don't believe that we should have to work for anything. In contrast to the father's generous attitude of "what's mine is yours," we have a greedy, selfish part of us that dares to proclaim the opposite, "what's yours is mine."

If you can't see this dynamic in yourself just now, perhaps you can see it in children you know. It is a common belief among children that they are the center of the universe. Parents live to serve the children, right? Not the other way around. Children believe that they should get what they want just because they want it, without any consideration for whether or not they truly need it, whether or not it would be good for them to receive it, and whether or not the parents have it to give. Children ring the butler's bell, which in baby-speak means crying, expecting that Mommy and Daddy will come running to satisfy their every need.

The older son's attitude is rarer. Though his respectful attitude hampers him in some ways, he understands that his father deserves his service, his devotion, and his responsibility. That is the proper order of things. As we grow into maturity, we discover and come to accept that we did not give birth to ourselves. I know that is a funny way of putting it, but I think it captures an important truth. Hopefully, like the older son, we come to understand that the right attitude toward our parents is gratitude. Our parents gave us our lives. Life itself is our inheritance. Our parents do not owe us anything. Yes, of course, we deserve to have our basic needs for care met by our parents. Because they have taken on the commitment of having children, they are responsible for feeding and tending us, keeping us safe, and equipping us for adult life. But beyond that, the rest is an undeserved bonus for which we ought to be grateful. And gratitude is not just a state of mind; it is a way of life.

An attitude of entitlement is a huge handicap in life. When we lack something we need or want, entitlement promotes resentment about it—unlike gratitude that promotes motivation to do something about it. Whereas gratitude is the attitude of active producers, entitlement is the attitude of passive consumers. As Jesus shows us in his story, entitlement leads to a wasteful, prodigal approach to life. When, instead, we see our inheritance as a gift subject to the giver's terms, we are motivated to appreciate and cherish it, to honor it, and to be responsible for it.

In Jesus' story, I think there is unique wisdom to be found in the father's response to his younger son. Rather than reacting to his son's selfish, reckless entitlement by retaliating in kind, the father maintains his own separate character. If it was within the character of the father to generously indulge the son's wish to discover lessons about life on his own, then it is also within the father's character to generously indulge his son's humble return. While there may be situations in which the father's approach might be unwise in real life (we can easily imagine them), the message of the story comes through. The father is a separate person. His way of dealing with his son's return is to be generous and forgiving. He loves his son. His heart is open. He realizes that his son's homecoming is a gift. And he receives it with gratitude.

I always feel grateful that this story doesn't forget the other end of the spectrum. If you're like me, you identify consciously more with the elder son than the younger. I like to see myself as the good, responsible child—never reckless, never wasteful, never taking my parents for granted. I work hard and try to make my parents proud. But I relate to the dark side of the older brother's character, too. I know what it's like to play the quietly suffering martyr. So often I back myself into the very same problematic corner that the younger son dove into headfirst. I wind up thinking that because of my good works, I am entitled to something in return.

Oh, this is a difficult lesson. Even when we are good, responsible children, we don't deserve anything more than if we were lazy, irresponsible ones. The inheritance isn't given because we deserve it or because we have earned it. It is given as a gift. It is given at the discretion of the giver. And if he chooses to give it to all of his children equally, regardless of their merit, then that is his right. And if he is a generous man, then that is exactly what he will do.

But there is compassion in this difficult lesson, too. I sense it from the father's response to his eldest son. Not only does he gently but firmly explain that it is his prerogative as the father to give as he sees fit, he also lets his eldest know that he wishes him to enjoy his inheritance. He does not want his son to suffer silently or to be miserly with himself or to work so hard that he is too tired to have a little fun. The father realizes that sometimes his son takes this responsibility business too far. "What's mine is yours," says the father. Life is meant to be enjoyed. That inheritance is available now. Enjoying it is part of honoring and cherishing it.

While sharing his wisdom about life, in Matthew 25:14–30 Jesus tells another story about how we ought to use the gifts we have been given. It takes an entirely different angle from the one taken in the Parable of the Prodigal Son.

The story goes that a man went away on a trip, leaving ten of his servants in charge of his wealth. He gave them each one talent to invest while he was gone. We can think of a talent in the ancient Near East sense as a sum of money—as Jesus meant it, literally—or we can think of it as a talent in our modern English meaning of the word—as I think is befitting of Jesus' meaning, too.

The servants all took their responsibility seriously. Some even took it enthusiastically. They traded, invested, bargained, and in all kinds of clever ways tried to make their talent work for them. All except one. One servant was too fearful to take the kind of risk that investment always brings. So he dug a hole in the ground and buried his talent there for safekeeping. You see, some of the servants—and even the neighbors—were suspicious of their master. They didn't like how powerful he had become. They just didn't trust him.

When the master came back from his journey, he checked in with his employees to see how they had handled his investments. The first guy said, "Master, I invested your talent and gained ten more."

His master replied, "Great job! You are a good and faithful servant. Because you have been faithful with a few things, I will put you in charge of many more. When I'm done with the accounting, let's go out and have a drink to celebrate."

The next fellow came in. "How did you do?" the master asked. The second fellow said, "Sir, you entrusted me with this talent. I invested it and gained five more."

His master replied, "Great job! You are a good and faithful servant. Because you have been faithful with a few things, I will put you in charge of many more. Later, I'm going out to celebrate our success. You should come."

Then, along came the fellow we're all a bit worried about. The master called him in and asked how he had managed his investment. Buried-it-in-a-hole guy said, "Master, I know that you are a mean and tightfisted man, expecting to get something back even when you did not invest it. I was afraid of what would happen if I invested the talent and lost it, so I decided that the safe bet was to make sure I had it all to give back to you. So I hid it in a hole to keep it safe. Here it is, just the same as when you left."

Well, this master had a different response to his servant than the father did to his prodigal son. Keep in mind that Jesus' parables are teaching stories—different story, different point. In this story, the master replied, "You wicked, lazy servant! So you knew that I would expect a return on my investment no matter what? Well then, at the very least, you could have put the money in a savings account at the bank and earned some interest. That's just common sense."

The master went on, "What am I going to do with you? Give your talent to the one who has ten. You wasted yours and cannot be trusted with it. At least we know he'll invest it properly. My lesson to you is this: Whoever has will be given more, and they will have more than they can imagine. Whoever does not have, even what they have will be taken from them. As for you, I have no use for you. Get out of here. You're fired!"

This is the kind of story that will get your attention. It might even get under your skin. That, of course, is what it is designed to do. We don't like the idea of a master who holds us to such strict account. We prefer one who is generous and gives us second and third chances. But Jesus is saying that there is a time and place for mercy and there is a time and place for accountability. Not only is our inheritance a gift to be received and enjoyed; it is a responsibility to be taken seriously.

It would be easy to take Jesus' Parable of the Talents in a concrete way, thinking that we will be rewarded if we take risks and work hard or, on the other hand, punished if we are frightened and lazy. But the parable is not really about punishment and reward. It is about more than that. It is about how things are. If we receive the gifts we have been given, whether these gifts are money, talent, or other kinds of symbolic wealth, and invest them thoughtfully and seriously, then we will reap rewards spiritually and emotionally. The gifts are meant to be used. They are valuable. They are a sacred trust. They are seed money for our lives. They are something we can—and should—build on.

But if, on the other hand, we receive the gift with fear and mistrust—as a burden rather than an opportunity—then we are inclined to turn away from it and not make the best use of it. In this state of mind, we can't think in a reasonable way about how to use our gifts because we are on our heels, living in fear, even a bit paranoid. After all, if we follow the story carefully, we are so suspicious that we can't even let the bank hold the valuables for us.

This kind of passive, mistrusting attitude becomes a self-fulfilling prophecy. The way that we go about managing our talents leads to the punishment itself. Like muscles, talents, when not used, atrophy. Like money, talents, when not invested, lose value. Like spiritual and emotional gifts, talents, when not used, are good for nothing. That's not punishment; that's just the gospel truth.

There is one more aspect of this parable that I find particularly insightful, and it carries an important psychoanalytic meaning. For each of the servants, the view of the master affected the view of the gift. The buried-it-in-a-hole servant viewed the master as tightfisted, punitive, and harsh. This was the same master who was viewed by the other two servants as generous and supportive. If we view our parents—real and symbolic—as punishing, criticizing, and cruel, then we are paralyzed. We cannot truly view the gift as a gift. Instead, it is felt to be a setup for failure. But if we view our parents as helpful figures who are there to get us started and to support us along the way, then we can take risks to use their gifts wisely and creatively.

As I said, most every wisdom tradition has a special focus on gratitude. For example, the Jewish tradition views thankfulness as a spiritual value. The more we practice thankfulness, the more we grow spiritually. The Hebrew term for gratitude is *hakarat hatov*, which literally means "recognizing the good." Such an orientation to life allows us to see the good that is there rather than to focus on what is missing. Such an orientation also helps us to cope with the difficulties of our lives because we know there is good that we can draw upon.

The more we practice thankfulness, the more we grow spiritually.

There is a story used in modern Jewish education to teach about the importance of gratitude. The story has become a kind of urban legend, rich with wisdom for those who wish to develop a more meaningful approach to life.

The story goes that the world-famous violinist Itzhak Perlman was playing a concert in New York City in the mid-1990s. Stricken with polio as a child, he wears braces on both legs and walks with two crutches. Even though walking is so difficult for him, he tenaciously made his stage entrance without additional assistance. The audience sat in awe and sympathy, watching him painfully enter and then cross the stage to his chair. He sat down slowly, placed his crutches on the floor, loosened the braces on his legs, and got into position to play. One had the sense that the man had overcome enormous odds. The hand that he was dealt in life had a card of musical brilliance, a card of physical adversity, and a card of perseverance. But he plays that hand like he is all in.

That night, like all other concert nights, Perlman tucked his violin under his chin and nodded at the conductor to begin. As he got into the piece—some versions of the story say he was just a few bars in and others say he was well into it—one of the strings of his violin broke. It was a snap so obvious that it couldn't be missed. Everyone thought that, surely, the momentum of the piece would be ruined, as he would have to stop to replace the string or borrow another violin—no easy task for even an able-bodied man.

After stopping the orchestra, the conductor looked over to see what Perlman wished to do. To everyone's surprise, Perlman raised a single finger to the conductor, a sign to wait just a moment. He closed his eyes, clearly gathering his thoughts. Then he opened them, looked at the conductor, and signaled him to go on. The orchestra took the conductor's cue, and off they went again as if they hadn't missed a beat. Only now, Perlman was playing on three strings.

Many people believe that this story must be a legend because it is impossible to play a symphonic work on violin with just three strings. But if anyone could, Itzhak Perlman could, right? One can imagine him working his way through the music around the missing string, compensating, adjusting, and improvising. It couldn't have been the same piece, of course. But it was brilliant, passionate, and beautiful. For the audience bearing witness to such a marvel, it was even better than what they had come to hear.

A local newspaper reported that when Perlman finished playing, the audience sat in stunned silence before leaping to their feet with an extraordinary outburst of applause. It was also reported that after the audience quieted down, Perlman wiped the sweat from his brow and said, "You know, sometimes it is the artist's task to find out how much music you can still make with what you have left."

I don't know whether or not this story actually happened, but I know that, in the psychological sense, it is true. The truth of the story is that Itzhak Perlman is showing us more than his attitude toward music; he is showing us his attitude toward life itself. Here is a man who knows all too well what it means to accept and work with limitations. He knows the undeniable truth that no matter how hard he works, he will never have it all. There will always be something missing—whether it is a string on the violin or the ability to walk with ease. But just as there always will be something missing, there always will be something left. Perlman decided to take the attitude that what is left is enough.

For me, these stories come together as if through a prism, illustrating the many dimensions of a single truth: We must recognize the good we have been given in life and make good use of it. The key to happiness is to recognize the good, to invest your talent, and to receive gratefully and responsibly the gifts you have been given. I can't think of a more winning strategy.

The Buddha's central idea comes around again. "Happiness is actually quite simple," he said. "The secret is to want what you have and not want what you don't have."

I think that's just right. Want the life you have, love it, cherish it, develop it, and use it. If you can embrace the life you have been given for the good that it is, then you can take it for a spin and see what it really can do.

This attitude is the antidote for one of the deadliest psychological poisons of modern times. Psychological health is poisoned by the mistaken belief that what is *missing* is the key to success. The most popular posts on my blog, *A Headshrinker's Guide to the Galaxy*, all explore this exact theme. We get stuck in the mistaken belief that the grass is greener on the other side of the fence. We are handicapped by the self-limiting perspective that our glass is half-empty rather than half-full. We are capsized by the toddler-style tantrum that life isn't fair.

If we open our eyes, we realize that life is difficult for everyone. True, it is more difficult for some than others. Not everyone gets dealt the same hand in life. We are not all created equal in that sense. Some receive more talents than others. Some inherit a whole lot of problems. Some are fortunate enough to have parents who are helpful and supportive, while others have parents who are neglectful or abusive. But as I have seen over and over again in my life and in my work, everyone has some good that they can use. Frankly, using whatever we have is the best any of us can do.

The attitude of gratitude is a shift that brings with it a new paradigm for successful living. If we view the good that we have as a gift, then we view our parents and the universe itself as generous and supportive. I mean this not in an idealistic sense, but in a realistic sense. Our parents and the universe do not give us everything we want or even sometimes need. But if we view them as giving us enough, then we can feel that we are safe and secure in their care. That kind of attitude helps us sleep at night and get up every morning.

This new paradigm also alters other views essential to successful living. Not only do we view what we have as good and as enough and as a gift, we view what we have as a personal investment plan. We shift from viewing ourselves in competition with others and instead as playing our own individual game. We do not have to keep up with the Joneses; we just have to do our best with what we have been given.

In this new paradigm, we view the life we have been given as a sacred trust, an inheritance for which we can and must be responsible. We honor our parents' legacy by faithfully using what they have given us. We are guided by a belief that they want us to use it in a way that enriches and fulfills our lives. We are at a great advantage in life when we imagine that our parents actually want us to succeed.

Can you imagine what your life would be like if you surveyed it with the eye of this new paradigm—if you looked over the landscape of your life and asked yourself, what good is here that I can use? What resources are available for me to invest? What have I been given that I can build upon? What is left that I can use creatively?

If you want to see the power of this shift, think about how it could change the pony and the shit story. A pony is a wonderful gift and, with a grateful attitude, you'd be able to appreciate it for what it is. But with an eye for the good, you might even be able to see the shit itself differently. After all, used in a creative way, even shit can help make things grow. It all depends on how you see it.

CHAPTER SEVEN

BECAUSE THINKING MAKES IT SO

On Thinking

WOVEN THROUGH EACH OF THE chapters so far is a basic principle that our attitude affects how we see and experience reality. Whether we call it a state of mind, a perspective, a point of view, a personal bias, or an unconscious inner world, we come to our lives with preconceptions that shape our reality. "Life is a creation of the mind," said Buddha. "What you see is what you get," quipped Flip Wilson's character, Geraldine Jones. And last, from Shakespeare's Hamlet, "There is nothing either good or bad, but thinking makes it so."

Thinking makes it so. The mind matters. While we don't have an influence over whether or not our thinking affects our experience of reality—it just does—we do have some influence over *how* it influences us. The good news is that, with effort, we can develop the mind so that it can help us deal with reality more effectively.

When it comes to thinking, we all start at the same place in life, relatively speaking. Just like we all are born with two eyes, a nose, and a mouth, we all are born with a rudimentary lens through which we view the world. This inborn lens is the pleasure-pain principle that we explored at the beginning of this book. We come into the world predisposed to think about our experiences as belonging to one of two categories: either pleasurable or painful, either good or bad. How we sort our experiences then dictates what we do about them. In this case, we seek what feels good and avoid what feels bad. That is the universal starting point on the journey to developing a mind.

With experience and effort, we develop and improve upon this rudimentary lens so that it becomes more and more refined, nuanced, and stable. We settle on our typical way of seeing things and it becomes, in essence, a personal frame of reference that we bring to all experiences, both old and new. For example, if we settle on a glass-is-half-full way of seeing things, then we are primed to give new experiences the benefit of the doubt as being good even before we meet them. If, on the other hand, we settle on a glass-is-half-empty approach, then even novel experiences are tainted from the get-go with a slightly negative sheen. Innocent until proven guilty; guilty until proven innocent. It all depends on the instructions your inner judge gives you.

Psychoanalysts have devoted themselves to trying to understand how these unconscious filters, lenses, or biases develop. We have discovered that, while we all have these unconscious filters, they differ from person to person based on a unique combination of biology, temperament, and early life experiences. Undoubtedly, one of the main psychological tasks of the first few months of life is to install and set up the mental equipment for thinking. As babies, not only do we need to learn how to nurse and sleep, we also need to learn how to think.

In studying how we learn to think, the first helpful insight I found is that we learn to think *out of confusion*. For a long time, I had the mistaken idea that the mind is like a calculator. You put in the numbers and it calculates the answer—simple as that. The problem with this model is that it makes you feel pretty stupid if you don't know the answer. It makes you feel even dumber if you don't even understand what the numbers mean or what you're supposed to do with them. But a lot of thinking starts out just like that. It starts in a state of confusion, with the need to make some meaning out of information that doesn't have any meaning yet.

Can you picture Rodin's famous sculpture, *The Thinker*? It is an enormous, strong figure of a man, sitting on a rock, chin resting on his hand, thinking. Some say he is thinking about the universe of heaven and hell. Others say he is thinking about creating his next brilliant poem. Whatever he is thinking, the image reveals the end, not the beginning, of a long process to develop the capacity to sit, reflect, plan, and make sense of a complex world.

The capacity to think begins in a state of confusion—more like a Salvador Dalí painting than a Rodin sculpture. At first, we don't know what things mean and we don't know how they go together. As babies, we are bombarded with all kinds of disturbing sensory input—sounds and shapes, light and dark, cool and hot, pain and pleasure. In the beginning, we have no idea what any of it means. But we have to figure it out, and there is a pressure to do so quickly.

The process of learning to think is no casual walk in the park, because our early confusion is inevitably linked to a feeling of danger. Helpless and vulnerable, we experience everything in an exaggerated form. The good is not just good; it is blissful and ideal. The bad is not just bad; it is horrendous and terrifying. Here is the second important insight that I want to show you. Not only do we develop the capacity to think *out of confusion*, but we do so *under pressure*. Life-and-death pressure, to be precise.

> *The process of learning to think is no casual walk in the park, because our early confusion is inevitably linked to a feeling of danger.*

Think about this experience as being a bit like the game of dodgeball. There are two teams, lined up on opposite sides of the gym. Half a dozen medium-sized balls are placed in the middle of the gym and, at the sound of the whistle, everyone runs to grab a ball and starts throwing it at a member of the opposing team. Your job is to hit someone else and avoid getting hit by someone else. If you're really ambitious, you might even try to catch a ball that is thrown at you and thereby eliminate your opponent. The scene is chaotic, dangerous, and pressured—balls flying everywhere, kids colliding into one another, and a general atmosphere of kill-or-be-killed. That's the kind of ambience in which the early mind is compelled to develop and figure things out.

So, here's what we do. We attempt to make sense of the information that is bombarding us by first trying to sort it out. We need to figure out what is good and what is bad. We need to figure out what is safe and what is dangerous. Just like in the old cowboy movies, we've got to figure out who's wearing the white hats and who's wearing the black hats. We've got to know whom to trust.

The psychoanalytic term for this sorting process is called *splitting*. The capacity to split, at first, is the baby's most helpful tool. If we can categorize our experiences as good or bad, pleasurable or painful, then we emerge out of confusion into clarity. The world becomes simpler. It becomes something we can think about. And once we can think about it, we can determine what to do. That's the second step.

Once we can categorize our experiences as good or bad, knowing what to do with them becomes a whole lot easier. Typically, we hold onto the good experiences and get rid of the bad ones. Psychoanalysts call these mental processes *introjection* and *projection*, respectively. We are at a great advantage in life when we can figure out the good stuff and take it in. Indeed, we are nourished and strengthened by the good and, furthermore, we feel protected and loved when we keep company with those who are good. On the other hand, we are also at a great advantage in life when we can figure out the bad and stay away from it. We do well in life when we can call a spade a spade, a poison a poison, and an enemy an enemy. If we can't sort things out accurately, then we wind up confused and inadvertently putting ourselves in harm's way.

Early mental life involves processing one experience after another through this rudimentary system. We develop a pretty reliable inner gatekeeper who is able to assess what is going on and what to do about it. Is it good? Keep it. Is it bad? Get rid of it. Over and over, we consider and sort, then decide what to do. Once we get the hang of this simple binary system, our world begins to settle down. It becomes less confusing. Anxiety recedes into the background. We feel safer and more secure. Now there is room to think in a more refined way.

At this point, though, things get even more interesting. Once you've mastered the art of black-and-white thinking, you begin to realize that the world is not actually as black-and-white as it seemed. Or, better said, it is not as black-and-white as you made it out to be. For example, you identified the one who cares for you as "good"; because Mom makes you feel good, she must be good. You also identified the one who does not come when you need her as "bad"; because Mom makes you feel bad, she must be bad. But then you begin to see that there's more to it. Upon closer inspection, it turns out that the one who makes you feel good and the one who makes you feel bad are *the same person*. Frankly, it boggles the mind.

Once you start looking for it, you recognize this phenomenon everywhere. The one who loves also disappoints. The one who hurts also helps. And not only do good and bad seem to live together in other people, they live together in you, too. In your own mind, you are an angel one moment and a devil the next. You are a murderer one moment and a lover of peace the next. These contradictions seem to live side by side, ushering in a new kind of confusion. How do you make sense of this new reality that does not conform to your well-established black-and-white way of viewing things?

It reminds me of our first day of German class when I was in eighth grade. Maybe you've had a similar experience. My new teacher, Herr Mahnken, rolls into class looking all distinguished and smart. He seems nice. But when he starts to speak, nothing he says makes any sense. Then it begins to dawn on me. He is speaking German. He is giving us a little preview of what we are going to learn in German class. Cool. But then he keeps speaking German. For fifty excruciating minutes. German and not a bit of English. Not a word I can understand. He is making me feel dumb. He is making me feel confused. What am I to think of him? What am I to do with him? In a way, I like him; he is going to be a challenging teacher. But in another way, I don't like him; he is making me feel small and stupid.

Now I have to make a decision. It is the same decision I had to make when black-and-white splitting was working so well. But now, the decision isn't so clear. Do I let him in? Or do I keep him out? Do I stay open to him? Or do I turn away?

These are the moments when mature thinkers are made. People who want to grow their minds will let him in and stay open. They will tolerate the uncertainty of not knowing if he is good or bad. Willing to risk it, they will give themselves more time and experience with the teacher. Perhaps with more information, it will become clearer whether or not Herr Mahnken can be trusted.

These are also the moments when immature thinkers are made. People who cannot stand the confusion, the feelings of smallness, and the uncertainty of not knowing will turn away. Confusion rattles them; frustration defeats them. They foreclose on the opportunity to have a good experience because they cannot stand the possibility that it might turn out badly. They don't give themselves a chance to develop more critical thinking capacity. Despite the mixed picture, they will make Herr Mahnken bad, committing themselves just a bit more to a lifetime of black-and-white thinking.

As you can probably guess, I gave Herr Mahnken a chance. He turned out to be a wonderful teacher and mentor. Over the next five years, I would stop by his office after school and talk about life, philosophy, religion, and music—in English, thankfully. I learned to speak German well enough that, while on a concert choir trip to Germany in my senior year of high school, I was able to converse with a group of children on a boat meandering down the Rhine River. One of our trip's chaperones, Herr Mahnken, looked upon the scene with pride.

We are fortunate when we have a parent, teacher, coach, or even a therapist who is able to usher us into the world of mature thinking. When we feel safe enough in their care, we can take the risk to move forward without knowing the outcome. When we feel encouraged by their support, we can try on new ideas and consider more complex realities. When we have someone who believes in us, we can stretch ourselves to grow our minds because we have hope that everything will be all right. We have some confidence that, even if we stumble along the way, it will not be the end of the world.

The world rarely conforms to black-and-white categories. It is shades of gray. Or maybe it is better to say that it is a Technicolor world. So much to see, so much to consider, and so many nuances to understand. The more we can let all aspects of that world in, the better we will be able to understand it. And the better we understand the world—both the outside world and the inside world—the better equipped we are to make good decisions and successfully navigate our way down the river of life.

It takes a lot of effort and courage to develop the capacity to think. It is not the easy way. So much of our modern culture is anti-mind. We don't want to think. When faced with complicated thoughts and feelings, we shut down. We sidestep what is painful or confusing. We look the other way. We deny. We project. We see what we want to see. Like ostriches, we bury our heads in the sand.

This way of thinking—or should I say, this way of *not* thinking—is very common, not just among babies but among people of all ages. Unconsciously, this anti-thinking strategy is designed to keep us protected from realities that we fear we cannot face. We prefer to keep things simplistic, even if our view remains narrow or limited or just plain wrong. Nowhere is this more prevalent than in politics and religion. We choose false assurances over ambiguity, weak dogma over sophisticated understanding. We are more comfortable when we can pin things down with certainty, even if it means we convict or vilify an innocent person. We demonize, idolize, ostracize, and stigmatize, bypassing the truths that lie in-between.

Sadly, our efforts to avoid thinking actually backfire, making life more, not less, difficult to understand and, therefore, to face. Lacking the full picture, we are unable to see what's what. We misperceive. We misjudge. We are misled. As a result, our choices are often misguided. Everyone suffers.

Successful living hinges on our ability to perceive reality clearly and to think about it. We must become more like scientists or, better yet, more like detectives (think Sherlock Holmes). Experts at observation and inductive as well as deductive reasoning, detectives utilize the very qualities that make for a strong mind in the psychoanalytic sense.

A good detective tracks down the facts rather than obscuring them. He views problems as mysteries to be solved, not nuisances to be avoided. He makes sense of things, attributes the right bit to the right person, and lets the evidence speak for itself. He is willing to admit when he is wrong. He can tolerate being confused. He allows himself to be surprised. He eliminates neither lead nor suspect before its time. He is an equal-opportunity judge; no one is protected or pigeonholed in his search. He is patient and open-minded. He seeks to understand the whole picture. Above all, he sides with the truth.

That is what real thinking is like. Real thinking doesn't come naturally, even though we're all preprogrammed to learn how to do it. It takes training and discipline. One might even say it is the central mission of parents with their children—to teach them how to think. Surely, it is the central mission of psychoanalysts with their patients. The most important work is to try to understand what on earth is really going on.

Real thinking doesn't come naturally, even though we're all preprogrammed to learn how to do it. It takes training and discipline.

We are at a great advantage in life when we can see the whole picture and think about it. If we are open to gathering together all of our experiences without prejudice, life becomes a puzzle to piece together rather than a catastrophe to avoid. We say to ourselves, here are all the pieces. We ask ourselves, how shall we put them together? The more we are able to take the good with the bad and the pleasure with the pain, the more we have reliable information to guide us. The more we can see that complexities, contradictions, and ironies are part and parcel of the whole, the more we can make sense of things. And the more we can make sense of things, the better we will do. Isn't that the whole point, after all?

Developing the capacity to think is inseparably linked to another important psychological capacity: the capacity to manage our feelings. You can't have one without the other. So, it is to feelings that we now must turn.

⌣

CHAPTER EIGHT

CAN'T LIVE WITH 'EM, CAN'T LIVE WITHOUT 'EM

On Feelings

FEELINGS ARE THE BOON AND bane of psychological life. They are the heart and soul that make life worth living as well as the troublemakers that wreak havoc and hold us back. Alongside learning to think, learning to deal well with our feelings is one of the most important psychological skills that we can develop. And it is challenging to do so. As the writer Louisa May Alcott put it so sweetly, "A little kingdom I possess, where thoughts and feelings dwell; and very hard the task I find of governing it well." As I like to say, a bit more crudely, "Damn feelings. Can't live with 'em, can't live without 'em!"

Intense feelings are just very hard to manage. Often, they feel too hot to handle. They put a kind of pressure on us to act and react in harmful, reckless, or unwise ways. Fired up by intense love, we want to run from it or jump headlong into it. Churned up by intense frustration, we want to punch the wall or throw in the towel. Lit up by anger, we want to hurt someone, anyone, even ourselves.

Then there's the other maddening dynamic we must face—our feelings confuse us. Love and hate collide. Fear and longing coexist. Desire, hope, and dread are all mixed up. We don't know what we feel. We don't know how to feel. We are paralyzed by confusion. We don't know which way to turn.

Because feelings are so overwhelming, we often have the misconception that the best way to deal with them is to get rid of them. We think of our feelings as a problem, a threat, a nuisance, and a bother. We imagine that life would be so much easier if we could just shut them down entirely, and for good.

Feelings fuel the engine of one's personality.

But that simply won't work. Feelings belong to us. And they know it. They know where they belong. So, like a lost dog, they find their way home. Like a tossed boomerang, they come careening back. And like a pressure cooker, the more you keep the lid on them, the hotter they get.

Whether we use projection, repression, suppression, or just plain denial, attempting to turn off our feelings is a strategy that eventually backfires. The one who quells anger is the one who later explodes. The one who denies sexual feelings winds up acting out in the shadows. The one who shuns love becomes tormented by what is missing. Simply put, we become preoccupied with the very feelings we are trying to avoid.

Getting rid of feelings not only backfires, but it also drains us of the psychological energy that makes life worth living. Feelings fuel the engine of one's personality. They are the source of motivation.

They are the energy, the vitality, the juice of life. Without them, our lives wouldn't have any personality or dimension or color. There wouldn't be any joy or creativity or fun. There wouldn't be you. There wouldn't be me. Without our feelings, nothing would really matter.

Think about the words we use to describe people who are cut off from their feelings: stoic, aloof, vacant, distant, or robotic. When we interact with such folks, we immediately have a sense that there is no "there" there. That's because getting rid of feelings is an all-or-nothing proposition. You can't pick and choose. If you try to get rid of your feelings, you must get rid of *all* of them. And if you get rid of all of them, you can't help but go flat.

These observations have been confirmed by research scientists, as well. Antonio Damasio,[15] an internationally famous neuroscientist, has made his career by studying the role that emotions play in our lives. His extensive research with people who have had damage to the frontal lobe of the brain gives us a hint about the critical role feelings play in healthy psychological functioning.

Damasio discovered that there is a strong mind-body or mind-brain connection and that many problems occur when this connection is disrupted. One of these problems involves our ability to access and make use of our feelings. Patients with particular types of frontal lobe brain damage are so cut off from their feelings that, even in extremely emotionally arousing situations, they are emotionally blank. What is interesting, however, is that they still have a logical, rational understanding of their psychological and social worlds. They know that they should feel something, but they just don't. They know that something is off, but they don't know what it is. While they perform well on intelligence and decision-making tests in the laboratory, they are lost in the real world. They have no clue about what is going on.

Damasio concluded that such patients struggle in the real world because they lack the important information that we normally get from our "gut feelings." Gut feelings are kind of like intuition; they give us an instantaneous sense about what we should focus on. They narrow the field, so to speak, helping us sort out the complex information with which we are bombarded in this dodgeball-like world of ours. What's going on here? What are the rules of the game? What should I do? Whom should I trust? Which way should I go? Gut feelings help us get our bearings.

Taken together, these observations reveal an important truth. Feelings help us think. They are critical in pointing us in the right direction, showing us what to focus on, and helping us sort out the good from the bad and the safety from the danger. Without them, we would be hopelessly lost in a sea of indecision. Without them, we couldn't connect in a meaningful way with ourselves or one another. This is what I mean by the idea that we can't live without our feelings. Even if we could be rid of them—which, short of a brain injury, tumor, or frontal lobotomy, we really can't—we wouldn't want to. Feelings provide information essential to thinking and relating. We simply can't live—I mean *really* live—without them.

———

Since we can't live without our feelings, we have to learn to live with them. This is one of the keys to living a satisfying life. We've got to develop the capacity to manage our feelings well.

Just as children need parents to help them learn to think, they need parents' help to learn to manage their feelings well. The same is true of patients and their analysts. Bombarded by thoughts that need a thinker, we need the help of another to grow a rational mind. Flooded by feelings that need a container, we need the help of another to grow an emotional mind. To be sure, the emotional mind is developed just like the rational mind, under pressure and out of confusion. But the process has another essential component that I wish to emphasize—the emotional mind can only develop in a lively relationship with someone who has an emotional mind more developed than our own.

Developing a strong emotional mind is an interactive process. By now, this will be easy for you to understand because you have learned that one of our typical strategies for coping with difficult feelings is trying to get rid of them. We need to be engaged meaningfully with someone who can gather up our castaway feelings and gently but firmly return them to us. Such engagement gives us the opportunity to learn to deal with our feelings ourselves.

As a first step in this interactive process, it may be useful to think of a parent or a psychoanalyst as being like a catcher in baseball, receiving unwanted feelings that a baby or a patient throws at them. The parent or analyst catches the feelings and then returns them to their rightful owner—the pitcher. By doing so, she says, "These feelings belong to you. Take them back. Learn to hold onto them yourself."

But we know it's not that easy. As a next step, we must factor in the confusion and pressure that are felt by the one throwing the ball. He is throwing away feelings that are distressing, upsetting, even frightening. That is why he is trying to get rid of them in the first place. He doesn't actually want them back. For him, this isn't pitching practice or a friendly game of catch. Just as I mentioned in the last chapter, this game begins as a cutthroat game of dodgeball.

In the young mind, the players in the feelings game are believed to be on opposing teams, not the same team. The toss is forceful, designed to be final. It is thrown with a clear message: "I don't want it; you take it." From the child's perspective, the point of the game is that no one wants to receive the ball. And if someone has the audacity to catch it, look out, because it's coming right back with the same kind of force with which it was delivered.

So if the ball of feelings is to be handled well, then someone needs to change the terms of the game. If the catcher returns the ball of feelings in the same way it was delivered—with pressure, as something unwanted and too difficult to handle—then the ball remains dangerous and will be resisted. Nothing changes. But if the catcher can receive the ball in a more open way, such as something that can be dealt with safely and capably, then she can return it without such distress and aggression. If she can do that, she can redefine the game.

But this is difficult to do. It is difficult for any of us to openly receive a ball of feelings when it has been thrown at us aggressively. When someone dumps on us, yells at us, blames us, or humiliates us, we can't help but experience it as a personal attack. You observe a mother trying to deal with her child who is throwing a tantrum in the grocery store. She may initially respond calmly and with gentle firmness, but under the pressure of her child's attacks the mother can lose control. She raises her voice, begins to throw back her own threats, barbs, and accusations. We all know intuitively that the mother's escalating distress only makes the situation worse. We feel for both mother and child. We know that they both will lose this game. By retaliating rather than containing, the mother reinforces the idea that the game of feelings is dangerous and deadly. She reinforces the idea that feelings are too hot to handle because she cannot handle them well herself.

Perhaps now you can see how crucial it is to be in relationship with someone who has the maturity to resist the urge to become defensive or to retaliate under the pressure of our attacks. We cannot learn to manage our feelings without someone mature like that in our lives. We all need someone who can receive our unwanted, castaway feelings with understanding and concern. We need someone who is not intimidated or frightened by our feelings. Their unexpected openness sends an important message to us. It communicates to us that our feelings are not too dangerous or too much to bear. It shows us that the catcher wants to play on the same team, not on an opposing team. Such receptivity changes the whole ball game. When our feelings are handled well by someone else, we begin to consider the possibility that we might be able to manage them well by ourselves.

So let's trace this metaphor back to its actual roots in infancy so that we can see how the emotional mind develops in real life. Simply put, we can only learn to handle our feelings well with the help of someone, usually our mother, who can handle feelings better than we can. When we are young, we experience feelings as having incredible power—power to overwhelm us, to send us over the edge, even to kill us. But mothers know that feelings don't actually have that kind of power. They are just feelings. If feelings are treated as just feelings, they lose some of their sway.

When a baby is crying bloody murder because he is cold, hungry, or tired, it is enormously helpful when his mother comes along, picks him up, and soothes him by saying, "I know it is upsetting. Oh, you feel like it is the end of the world. But it's not. Everything's okay. I'm here. Let's see if we can figure this out together." She communicates to her baby that she understands his feelings and how powerful they seem to him. She communicates that she has a different understanding of them, that she views his feelings as just feelings. And as feelings, they can be safely experienced, understood, and handled in a manageable way.

Our mother's capacities to receive, understand, and gently but firmly return our feelings to us are perhaps her greatest legacy. An emotionally capable mother deserves our gratitude and respect because she does for us what we cannot yet do for ourselves. She receives our communications and understands them. She receives our upset feelings and contains them. She bears our anger without retaliation. She brings her more mature mind to our baby distress without falling apart (at least most of the time). She models for us what it looks like to be open to our feelings, to think about them, and to deal with them in an effective way. She works with us—bit by bit, step by step—to help us learn to be receptive to our own feelings, too, and so develop the capacity to deal with them ourselves.

As anyone will tell you, it isn't easy to be this kind of mother. The good news is that mothers don't need to be perfect in order to help us grow our minds. As psychoanalyst Donald Winnicott would say, all we need is a good enough mother. We need a mother who genuinely tries, who is successful some of the time, who gets help when she needs it herself, and who will make reparations with us when she lets us down. If we have that kind of mother as a model, we have a good chance of becoming that kind of person ourselves. And that's about as good as it gets; and that's plenty good enough.

As you can imagine, the extended training of psychotherapists of all kinds, and psychoanalysts in particular, is dedicated to becoming this kind of open, receptive, nonjudgmental, nonretaliating, and disciplined emotional container. Our patients need us to be that kind of container for them when they can't be it for themselves. The goal is that, over time and through experience with us, our patients can become that kind of container for themselves.

Through my years of experience on both sides of the psychoanalyst's couch, I have learned some surprising truths about feelings that I had never understood before. I have learned these truths not so much as theories but as living realities, having discovered them in the crucible of interactive experiences like I just described. Here are a few of the lessons I learned:

1. **Feelings are not the same as facts.** Just because you feel hurt doesn't mean you are being hurt. Just because you feel depressed doesn't mean there is good reason to be depressed. Just because you feel love doesn't mean the relationship is good for you. We have the mistaken idea that what we feel must be the truth, kind of like the mistaken idea that what we say when we are drunk must be the truth, too. But feelings are just feelings. While they do provide useful information, they do not tell the whole story.

2. **Feelings are not the same as actions.** Just because we have murderous feelings doesn't mean we have actually killed anyone. Just because we feel erotic desire doesn't mean we have had premarital sex or an extramarital affair. Similarly, just because we feel something doesn't mean we have to do it. Feelings can just be; they don't have to be converted into action.

3. **You can feel more than one feeling at the same time.** This lesson was such a surprise to me. I always thought that you could only feel one thing at one time. If I was mad, I couldn't feel love and understanding, too. If I was happy for someone, I couldn't be envious of them, too. If I wanted to be with someone, I couldn't want to be alone, too. It was very liberating for me to realize that emotional life is complex and that even contradictory feelings can coexist.

4. **Feelings are neither good nor bad, they just are.** Because of the way that the mind works, we have all sorts of disturbing, unwanted, violent, and sexual feelings. We often are judgmental toward these feelings in ourselves, even ashamed of them. But it is important to understand that these feelings—as feelings—are normal. How we think about them and what we do with them is what tells the tale.

Understanding the nature of our feelings helps us understand what needs to be done to manage them well. To be successful in life, we must bring our feelings together with our thinking.

You can't have one without the other. The emotional mind and the rational mind come together in the mature psyche in what psychologist Marsha Linehan calls "wise mind."[16]

Wise mind is the capacity to bear our feelings without acting on them. It is the basis of self-control. Wise mind is the capacity to reflect on our feelings and learn from them. It is the basis of self-knowledge. Wise mind is the capacity to integrate all the aspects of ourselves into a unified whole. It allows us to put feelings in their place, not as masters but as servants to a greater good. It allows our rationality to be in its place, too, not as a data-processing machine but as a disciplining guide to our emotional liveliness.

Wise mind is the capacity to reflect on our feelings and learn from them.

There is a wonderful scene in the movie *Seabiscuit*, the story of a thoroughbred racehorse that had a slow, rough start in life before becoming an amazing champion. In an early scene in the movie, the horse owner's wife and trainer are watching Seabiscuit in practice as he wildly tears around the track. It is easy to see how fast this horse is, but there's a problem. He's all over the track; he doesn't seem able to run in one direction.

We're all just like Seabiscuit in the beginning. With uncontained feelings as our guide, we too run in every direction. But if our feelings are trained with gentle but firm discipline, we have the chance to move forward in a truly spirited way. It is no wonder this was the very metaphor Sigmund Freud used nearly a century ago when describing the successful integration of all aspects of the psyche. Like a rider trains and makes use of the vitality of a horse, a mature person disciplines and makes use of the reservoir of his or her passions and feelings. If we can develop the capacity to manage our feelings well, then maybe we will not only learn to live with them, but we will no longer be so keen to live without them.

CHAPTER NINE

EVERYONE IS WELCOME AT THE TABLE

On Balance

THESE IDEAS ABOUT HEALTHY PSYCHOLOGICAL life are certainly not new, but they are unusual in this day and age. In today's psychological climate, it seems strange to consider the idea that we can make our lives better by doing something different with what we already have. We hear reverberations of the same theme over and over again: integration, acceptance, compromise, making peace. To put it in a new way, the atmosphere of a healthy inner world is balance.

I approach my life and my practice with a basic assumption. It is an assumption that I cannot prove scientifically, even though it proves itself over and over again to me through experience. I believe that the sum total of what we have and who we are is enough to work with. The good, the bad, and the ugly within each of us are the raw materials from which we can build a satisfying life. Nothing more is needed, nor can we do with less. We must work to find balance with all of who we are—finding a place for all of the conflicting impulses, attitudes, thoughts, and feelings that we naturally have as the divided selves that we naturally are.

In finding balance, we must come to understand that we have a complex inner world made up of competing views and voices, sometimes in harmony with one another but often at odds. The "you" who sets the alarm to wake up early is the same "you" who groans when it rings, turns it off, and goes back to sleep. The "you" who agrees to take on a new challenge is the same "you" who procrastinates in actually doing it. The "you" who loves is also the "you" who hates. The "you" who feels smart, competent, and capable is also the "you" who feels insecure, silly, and dumb. And the list goes on.

Conflicting impulses toward health, growth, love, work, and reality live together, side by side, inside us.

Here's the good news—these inner contradictions are completely normal. Conflicting impulses toward health, growth, love, work, and reality live together, side by side, inside us. Aggression and desire, envy and gratitude, hope and dread are roommates in the inner world. The task of psychological development is to get these opposing parts of ourselves in a dialogue with one another, negotiating a peaceful way of living together. Just as the prophet heralds the day when the wolf shall lay with the lamb in a future world of peace, so we work toward the day when our inner angels and demons live together in a more harmonious way. This peaceful coexistence of all the different parts of the psyche is a metaphor for building a satisfying, well-balanced psychological life—both on the inside and on the outside.

Unfortunately, at first we do not tend to deal with the complexities of our inner world by working toward balance, harmony, and inner peace. We can only learn this more mature approach with great effort and training. Instead, we typically approach these inner conflicts in the exact opposite way. We deal with the bad and ugly parts of ourselves with the same doomed approach that we use in dealing with unwanted feelings: We try to get rid of them.

I had a patient once who was very honest about his limitations and weaknesses, genuinely wanting my help to deal with them. But the process of dealing with them was torturous because whenever I spoke of his weaknesses, he would cry out, "Bad, bad, bad!" He immediately chastised himself for them (or felt I was chastising him for them), and rather cruelly, I might add. He hated these weaker parts of himself and wanted to be completely rid of them. There was talk of psychological exorcism, surgical removal, suicide, and murder. And he wasn't kidding. He wanted those parts G-O-N-E.

I had another patient who had a different but equally ill-fated tack in dealing with the parts of himself that he despised. He had plans to replace those unwanted parts of himself with admired parts of other people. Over the course of time, he vividly described the ideal man that he wanted to become and, in his mind, it was my job to help him become that man. Now he was a reasonably good-looking, intelligent, friendly, and generous guy. But his own good qualities weren't good enough for him. He wanted to have the good looks of George Clooney, the intelligence of Steve Jobs, the interpersonal skills of Oprah Winfrey, and the servant's heart of Mother Teresa. Anything less made him feel terribly inadequate and miserably depressed. In a way, he knew that becoming this ideal was impossible, but in another way, he was utterly serious that this should be his goal. He couldn't just become a better version of himself; he wanted to become a patchwork of the very best parts of the very best people he could imagine.

We can relate to the states of mind in both of my patients. What do I want to be when I grow up, we ask? Loving, capable, rich, smart, strong, wise, generous, kind, clever, successful, humble, confident, funny, respectful, and the list goes on. What do I *not* want to be when I grow up? Lazy, greedy, envious, arrogant, slow, stupid, selfish, and on and on. We want to hold onto the best and get rid of the worst of ourselves. But some of us aren't even satisfied then. We want more—not just the best parts of ourselves but the most appealing qualities of others, too. I shudder to think of the monster you or I would become if such a fantasy could ever come true—phony, too perfect, and absolutely impossible to live with.

Lucky for us, psychological life doesn't work that way. Just as there are some desired experiences that are against the laws of physical nature (for example, thanks to gravity, you can't go up and down at the same time), some apparently appealing experiences are simply against the laws of psychological nature, too.

I have a saying that psychological matter is a lot like physical matter: It is indestructible. I can't prove this to you, but I'm pretty sure that it's true. I believe that you can't destroy anything in the mind. I'm serious. I really don't think you can. The contents of your mind—your thoughts, feelings, fantasies, and character strengths and flaws—belong to you forever. You can change their form or location, but they're still there. You can lock them in a closet, hide them under the bed, project them into someone else, and pretend they don't exist, but they're still there. That's really what the idea of the unconscious is all about. It's the holding pen for all the unwanted parts of ourselves that we are trying to get rid of. We could say that it's a kind of burial ground, except all the corpses are still alive.

Another of my so-called laws of psychological nature is that efforts to get rid of parts of the self actually increase their power. There is an incredible segment in the animated Disney film *Fantasia* where Mickey Mouse is cast in the lead role of "The Sorcerer's Apprentice." If you haven't seen this nine-minute jewel or haven't seen it for a while, you might want to check it out because it is a remarkable illustration of the very laws of psychological nature that I'm talking about.

In the film, young Mickey Mouse is filled with envy over the Sorcerer's magical powers and frustrated with his position as a lowly apprentice, fit only for schlepping buckets of water. He hates his powerlessness and wishes to have the power of the Sorcerer. So when the Sorcerer steps away, Mickey puts on his master's magical hat and picks up his magical broom, pretending to take on the powers that he finds so appealing and irresistible. What does he do with this magic? No surprise; he casts a spell so that the broom becomes the bucket-schlepping loser-apprentice that he now controls.

Instantly, the broom comes to life and takes on the apprentice's unwanted task and identity, while Mickey Mouse looks on with self-satisfied superiority. In his smugness, however, Mickey falls asleep and things really get out of hand. Unsupervised, the brooms and the buckets multiply, creating a flood of water that threatens to drown them all. As the music swells, so does the chaos of the scene.

The flood becomes more and more menacing and overwhelming. His magical experiment has backfired, and Mickey is now more powerless than ever.

Just when Mickey is about to be swept away in the deluge, the Sorcerer returns with his true power and sets the situation right again. The water recedes, the buckets and brooms return to normal, and Mickey melts into a puddle of shame and guilt. After receiving a disciplining look and a gentle swat on the butt from the Sorcerer, Mickey slinks off to his bucket-schlepping duty, now feeling lowlier than ever.

As the film illustrates, by trying to get rid of unwanted parts of ourselves, we actually make things worse rather than better. Like a thrown boomerang, disowned parts of the self tend to come flying right back at us. I have a theory that they come back with extra force because they don't like being treated so badly. They don't appreciate being treated like they are worthless trash, fit only for the rubbish heap. Lock an unruly child in a closet, and what does he do? Bang and scream and kick and shout until you let him out so he can have his say. Even so-called "bad" parts of the self have feelings, too.

When your approach to dealing with yourself is fueled by hatred, rejection, and prejudice, it's bound to fail. When you look at some aspect of yourself and say, "You're bad, rotten, and good for nothing," you are attacking yourself. And a life that is based in self-hatred, by definition, cannot be a very satisfying or happy one.

In working toward a better life, we've got to think about the kind of psychological culture we want to set up inside. What do we want the social rules to be? So many of us have a way of operating that is more akin to a cruel totalitarian regime, with ruthless leaders who rule with harsh judgment. Like *Alice in Wonderland*'s Queen of Hearts, our internal rulers are quick to pronounce the death sentence for the most minor and innocent of offenses, condemning our weaker selves with the cry, "Bad, bad, bad!" and "Off with their heads!" Hopefully, we can begin to question if that is really how we want to treat ourselves.

The good news is that, through disciplined psychological work, we can develop a healthier inner culture. We can modify how we treat ourselves. We can set up an internal regime that is governed by more benevolent leaders who listen to all citizens and exercise judgment with fairness. We can learn to be kinder to ourselves.

When I think of a balanced internal world, I think of making space for all aspects of the self to have their say and to have their place. I picture the internal world like a lively family with children and adults of all ages, seated around a table having a meal. Sometimes it is chaotic and noisy, as is the nature of complex family interactions. But a balanced internal world has a kind of orderliness in which the mature parts of the self are in charge of the less mature parts of the self, managing the little ones with concern and care but with discipline as well. An

. . . a balanced internal world has a kind of orderliness in which the mature parts of the self are in charge of the less mature parts of the self, managing the little ones with concern and care but with discipline as well.

internal mother and father preside over the family table, helping everyone to be heard, encouraging everyone to behave themselves and to get along.

Developing the mature internal parent parts of ourselves tends to be the key in setting up a healthier internal psychological culture, for the internal parents set the tone for how the family will operate. For an example of a good model, you only have to think about what Mary Poppins did for the Banks family—the rowdy children, Jane and Michael, with their well-intended but hopelessly ill-equipped parents. Or, at the other end of the spectrum, think about what *The Sound of Music*'s Maria did for the seven Von Trapp children who had been so terribly constrained by their strict and lonely father, the Captain. These mother figures swept in with a balance of benevolent discipline, loving attentiveness, and sense of joy that brought out the best in the children as well as the parents. We would all do well to grow that kind of nanny inside.

If those examples don't do it for you, think of Coach Buttermaker in *The Bad News Bears* or Principal Joe Clark in *Lean on Me* or Sister Deloris in *Sister Act* or pretty much any coach in a baseball or football movie that has a happy, tear-jerker ending.

You look at the early scenes of these films with the chaos, the incompetence, the laziness, and the disobedience, and you think, how is anyone going to do anything constructive with these kids or players? And then they do. That's a little bit like what the internal world is like. If we are honest, we realize that we are all Bad News Bears in training. We've all got a motley crew of characters inside who need some help pulling together. And, metaphorically speaking, we need an internal coach or a principal or a nanny who believes in us and listens to us enough to call out the best in us.

These are, of course, everyday examples of very profound dynamics. The internal parents draw disparate parts of the self together, and this is no easy task. They are part secretary of state, camp counselor, and kindergarten teacher. They bring a rowdy bunch of immature parts of the self into a functioning unit where no one is excluded, where bullying is addressed, where the quiet ones are supported as they find their voices, and where the life-giving aspects of the group are encouraged for the common good. Because the internal family that I am describing is real, it is therefore never ideal. Like any well-functioning family, it is always a work in progress.

Just as you cannot really destroy, get rid of, or take away anything from the psyche, I also believe that you cannot create something totally new. Psychoanalyst Betty Joseph impressed this idea upon me. In her fifty years of studying how people change in psychoanalysis, she came to believe that the best we can do is give strength to weaker parts of the personality that are already there. The silenced, frightened, vulnerable parts of ourselves need our attention. We must fan the embers, so to speak, of what already lies within us.

In my experience in psychoanalysis, it takes people a while to get the gist of this new model. It is so counterintuitive. It takes a lot to give up on the idea that the best thing to do with the problematic aspects of ourselves is to squelch them. It blows the mind to think that the opposite could actually work. Shine a light on our problems? Give our fears and insecurities a microphone? Get to know and even embrace our castaway selves? Surely no good could come of that.

But, bit by bit, people begin to see. Change is a change of direction. It is a change of how we go about doing things. It is a rebalancing, a recalibration of what is already there.

There is something profoundly reassuring about this idea. It means that you already have what you need in order to develop a more satisfying life. You don't need to go out and buy it; you don't need to steal it from someone else. You are the raw material. The work of personal growth is not new construction; it is a remodeling project. Weaker parts can be reinforced, repaired, and spruced up. More dominant, problematic parts can be softened, disciplined, and refined, placed more in the background rather than taking up center stage. Psychological growth is about reorganizing the inner world, not changing it entirely. We don't create something altogether new; we work with what is already there.

The work of personal growth is not new construction; it is a remodeling project.

I like this model because it rests on a foundation of appreciation, respect, and love for all aspects of who you are. It tempers self-hatred with tolerance. It softens judgmentalism with grace. It views change as fundamentally constructive rather than destructive. It takes as a starting point the belief that you are enough.

For some, this is a liberating model for an additional reason. Many people have a built-in distrust of psychotherapists—and psychoanalysts, in particular—because they think that we're going to try to change them. At first blush, this is kind of an odd concern, since people are usually going to a psychotherapist because they want to change. But there is a deeper fear that is reflected in this idea, and one that we should take seriously. We all have a healthy, protective attitude toward our identities. We don't want someone making us into someone we are not. So some people take it as good news when I tell them that, in the most fundamental ways, they will always be who they are. All that therapy can do is make some adjustments—adjustments that could change their lives in dramatic ways, yes, but still, mere adjustments.

One day, several years into her treatment, a patient said to me out of the blue, "You lied to me." Drawing on my most sophisticated professional vocabulary, I replied, "Huh?" She said, "At the beginning, you said that change in psychoanalysis would be a small change, like adjusting the course of a ship a few degrees. But I feel like the changes you are asking me to make are enormous!"

This was an important moment of clarification, brought to the surface with real passion. Yes, change in psychoanalysis feels enormous. It takes huge amounts of effort, courage, and surrender to be different from how you have always been. It takes commitment of time, money, and discipline that few can afford. It is hard, hard work. I said this to my patient. Then I went on, "But let me ask you something. Are you fundamentally the same person you were when you started? Are you still *you*?"

She could see what I meant. She could see it both ways now. There is a paradox in the reality that we change greatly, yet we don't really change fundamentally. Take me, for example. I've been through many years of psychotherapy and I've made significant changes in my life for which I am extremely grateful. But I look back at photos of myself as a child, or hear descriptions of myself from my parents, or reminisce with old friends, or read progress reports from my first-grade teacher, and I think, "Yep, that's me. Still the same Jen. Just a different package now." Much of who we were at birth, age three, age seventeen, age thirty, endures. We shape, we reorganize, we refine, but we still retain our essential character.

In addition to feeling some relief at this idea, it's also easy to feel disappointed. As much as we don't want to be made into someone else, many of us actually wish we *could* be made into someone else. Sometimes we're just so tired of ourselves that we'd like to throw it all out, start fresh, and become someone altogether different. But it just doesn't work that way. All we have is who we are.

This idea about balance is both bitter and sweet. By accepting life's limitations, we gain access to its real possibilities. By forsaking the false paths, we choose a real path that leads to a better way of being who we already are.

I recently saw a New Year's resolution posted on Facebook that captures this notion well: "This year, I will do all that I can, with whatever I have, wherever I am . . . and I'll let good enough be good enough." Can you imagine what such a change of perspective could do for our lives?

The model of internal balance extends to our lives in the external world. It can have a positive influence on how we find balance both in our commitments and in our relationships with other people.

If you are like me, you struggle mightily in finding balance in your commitments. So often we are preoccupied by a mission to have it all. We want to have success in the workplace as well as in home life. We want to work less but make more. We want to eat and drink whatever we wish and still be healthy and fit. We want to have a weekend filled with rest and relaxation while hitting every party, family gathering, sporting event, and home-repair project. We don't want to let any opportunity pass us by.

But commitments in life inevitably involve trade-offs. This is true whether you live a balanced life or not. You can't be busy and relaxed at the same time. You can't be healthy and eat whatever you want. You can't accept every social invitation and have plenty of time for yourself. You can't be a working mom and have the same amount of time and energy for your kids as those moms who work exclusively in the home. You can't be a mom who works exclusively in the home and have the same satisfactions as a career woman. It's either one or the other or something in between. Yes, you can have some of each of these experiences over a lifetime; but that's not the same thing as having it all.

People hate it when I point out this reality. It is another one of those hard-to-stomach laws of psychological nature. There really is no free lunch. You can't get something for nothing. Life is a series of trade-offs. This truth is not necessarily a bad thing; it just is. If we can accept this essential reality, we become less encumbered by unrealistic expectations that lead to envy, frustration, and resentment. I know I keep coming back to this theme, but it is worth repeating. If we accept that we cannot have it all, we have a better chance of enjoying what we actually have.

So if you want to have a balanced external life, you've got to develop the chops for discernment. You've got to learn to say yes to some things and no to others. Becoming more selective involves a deepening of some commitments and a lessening of others. It is both gain and loss. We make choices that suit us for this time and season of our lives, and we let other things go.

This is hard for us. It is hard for us to willingly choose to do without something good, especially if we could have it. For example, I have chosen to make my relationship with my husband a priority; this means I have less time for my friends. I hate that. I also have chosen to be guided in my professional life by the principle of "do a few things well." This means I have to say no to a lot of great opportunities. I hate that, too. I look at other people who have a wide circle of friends whom they really enjoy, and I feel envious. I look at some of my colleagues who are teaching, speaking, publishing, and traveling around the country and the world, and I feel envious of them, too. On my better days, I feel satisfied and at peace with my choices. Other days, I am steamed that they come with such a cost. That's how balance goes.

There's another side to this dynamic. A balanced life not only involves making decisions about what we choose to take on; it also involves doing our best to deal with whatever comes our way, even those challenges we would not willingly choose. Death, illness, loss, and all sorts of other unwelcome experiences confront everyone at points along the way. Difficult people, trying circumstances, and unfair treatment are part and parcel of real life. So we must learn to deal with them, to roll with them, and to take them as they come. Like unwanted parts of ourselves, these unwanted aspects of our external lives demand our attention, our concern, and our care.

When you step back and look at the big picture, you begin to realize that one way or another every aspect of life is colored by challenges and complications—even the things we love and willingly choose, such as friendship, marriage, parenting, career, school, writing books, and making music or peace or even love. Just like the internal world is divided in its basic nature, so is the external world. Everything that is real involves some measure of conflict, disappointment, and distress. That is the balance of things. When we approach these inevitable conflicts with acceptance, grace, and determination, we have a greater chance of developing some measure of peace and harmony.

It is also a challenge to develop balance in our external lives, because we have to deal with other people. As my analyst often says with a heavy sigh, "People are hard." This is a pithy saying but one that couldn't be more true. Of course, there are lots of difficult people we must deal with in our personal and professional lives, whether that person is our spouse, parent, or child; coworker, boss, or employee; contractor, IRS agent, neighbor, or the guy who cuts us off on the freeway. But sometimes it's even hard to deal with the easy ones. Even people we love and admire and respect have different points of view, competing needs, and ways of thinking that are completely foreign to us. If we have developed more tolerance and patience with the competing parts of ourselves internally, we have a much better chance of being successful in dealing well with complex relationships with others.

Our approach to dealing with unwanted aspects of our internal lives is a key to success in the outside world. If we know how to negotiate peace with competing parts of ourselves, we have a pretty good idea about how to set the stage to facilitate peace with others. We do well to welcome differences with openness, goodwill, and thoughtfulness. When we accept our enemy as our brother, we have a much better chance of finding balance and compromise. When we find the commonality, listen with a genuine effort to understand, and view ourselves as being on the same team, we have a much better chance of finding a way to live together.

Just like the internal world, the external world becomes more balanced when an attitude of friendly openness toward one's enemy prevails. Peace treaties of all kinds have been negotiated on the golf course, on a weekend retreat in the mountains, or over a shared meal. When someone unwanted shows up for dinner, it's best to set another place at the table.

Hopefully you now can see this oscillating synergy between balance in the internal world and balance in the external world. The more we can approach our inner conflicts with kindness, fairness, and tolerance, the more we can take such a balanced approach to our conflicts in the outside world. The mature internal parents who preside over the internal family table are the same mature parents who negotiate conflicts with our commitments and with people in our external lives. And the more we are able to successfully negotiate conflicts in our external lives, the more confident and capable our internal parents become. One experience feeds the other, and we become stronger because of it.

As the ancient saying goes, there is a time and season for everything under heaven. All of the different parts of ourselves can have a welcome place at the table. But it's up to us to help them all get along.

CHAPTER TEN

YOU DON'T HAVE TO THROW OUT THE BABY WITH THE MANGER

On a Mind of One's Own

HOPEFULLY, YOU ARE BEGINNING TO understand how the inner world influences the outer world and, with that understanding, the importance of developing mature internal parents who can help you make your way through life. But I also guess that there is a burning question on your mind: How on earth do you develop these mature internal parents? As you become more and more interested in this idea of strengthening and developing your internal world, you've got to be wondering how to do it.

I wish I could whip out my handy-dandy how-to guidebook and give you the seven easy steps to developing mature parents in the internal world. But as you've figured out by now, that's just not how it works. All I can do is point you in the right direction and teach you a few principles to live by, and off you must go to find your own way.

Come to think of it, that pretty much sums up the essence of what I know about developing mature internal parents. Of course, you know that I'll elaborate—but still, what I just said is pretty much it. You've got to find someone who will point you in the right direction, who will teach you a few principles to live by, and who will send you off to find your own way.

So the simple principle of how-to-develop-mature-internal-parents is this—you've got to find some mature external parents first. You've got to turn toward reliable, wise, and helpful external parental figures and then sit at their feet, learn from them, and grow to be like them. Just as the internal world influences the external world, so the external world influences the internal world.

These external parental figures might be actual parents, grandparents, big brothers or sisters or uncles or aunts, or people who just feel like family. They might be teachers, coaches, sponsors, mentors, therapists, pastors, or other kinds of spiritual masters who you sense are the real deal. However you find them or perceive them, they are the higher power upon whom you depend and to whom you aspire. To grow psychologically, you must do all that you can do to find the good parents, get connected to them, and then depend on them to help you grow yourself—first from the outside in and then from the inside out.

Finding such parents is just the first step. Once connected to these wise ones, you must open yourself to all that it means to be in a real, authentic relationship with them—and that means you have to ride the roller coaster of loving them and hating them, admiring them and disdaining them, wrestling with them and leaning on them. It is a tumultuous process.

There is a famous story in the book of Genesis about such tumultuous engagement in the life of the young man Jacob—maybe you remember the rebellious, sneaky, precocious, and brilliant twin brother of Esau whom I used as an example to make another point in Chapter One. Many years after stealing his father's blessing from his brother, Jacob had the opportunity to receive that blessing on more legitimate terms. Having left home to make his own way, Jacob discovered that he could not really do so until he dealt with some unfinished psychological business. He needed to make amends to his brother.

So he took the journey back home with his new family by his side, nervous and unsure of the reception he would receive. On the eve of his homecoming, Jacob took some time to be alone, only to find himself in a wrestling match with a stranger in the middle of the night. Whether you think of what follows as a real event, a dream, or a myth—and his opponent as just some guy or an angel or a manifestation of God or Wisdom or the deep truth of Jacob's own unconscious mind—there is something profound to be learned from their encounter.

Jacob and the stranger were evenly matched, the fight nearly a draw. Pinned down and weary after fighting into the early hours of the morning, the man asked Jacob to let him go. Jacob replied in utter seriousness, "I will not leave you until you bless me." Scoundrel that he was, Jacob had no right to ask for a blessing or to insist it or to claim it. But this time he asked for it in all honesty, without guile. Along with a humbling pinch to the hip, the man gave Jacob what he asked for, and gave it to him for the right reasons. The man, the angel, or perhaps God-in-the-flesh blessed Jacob for struggling. Not for defeating him per se, but for engaging in a real and genuine struggle.

Jacob was on a psychological journey to learn to struggle like a man. We know that he could struggle like a baby, grasping his brother's heel before he even took his first breath. And we know that he could struggle as a rebellious teenager, stealing his brother's birthright through cunning and deceit. And if you know the rest of the story, you know that Jacob had a long and bumpy ride, mostly because of his own doing.

But this was a season in which Jacob was learning to struggle in a more mature way. He was beginning to listen to his dreams, to his inner voice, perhaps even to his God. He was going home to take responsibility for his failures, to face his brother whom he had wronged, and to try to make amends. That is the journey of evolving maturity that we would all do well to travel on. The stranger in the night honored this struggle and recognized that Jacob had changed. No longer a child, he had become a man. This was so apparent that the stranger believed Jacob had earned both a blessing and a new name; Jacob now would be known as Israel. The son had become a father, mature enough to become the father of a nation. And, no surprise, Jacob's new name means "he who struggles with God."

Life-changing, inner transformation only comes out of a sincere wrestling with one's good parental figures. This process often happens through struggle with our external parental figures, and it always involves an internal struggle, too. As Jacob discovered, growing up is a painstaking process that involves taking in the wisdom of your parents, fighting it, rejecting it, and taking it back again. He learned through experience that you've got to leave home in order to return home. You can take what your parents give you, but it only feels like it truly belongs to you when you feel that you have their blessing.

In this chapter, I will do my best to describe this unfolding process of developing a mind of one's own. For the sake of clarity,

I will break the process down into three phases, borrowing from British psychoanalyst Donald Meltzer's model. He wrote: "The paradox remains that the best aspect of the mind is beyond the self and the self must evolve in its relation to its internal objects through dependence, ripening to obedience, and ending as the acceptance of inspired independence."[17]

From the first to the last of our days, we live in a fundamental relationship with our parents, most especially the versions of our parents that live in the internal world. The key is to learn to use them properly, to evolve in our relationship with them. We first depend on our parents, although that is the beginning, not the ending of the journey. We then must learn to obey them, to take in what they have to give to us, and to learn to do it by ourselves. Only then can we develop the kind of real independence that involves being inspired by them to grow beyond them. That is really what I mean by maturity, an ever-evolving process of developing a mind of one's own.

PROPER DEPENDENCE

Like many other living creatures, human beings are biologically designed to depend on their parents in order to develop and learn to fend for themselves. This instinct is essential for survival. But while the period of dependency for some animals lasts for only a few days or weeks, humans depend on their parents for a rather long time— for more than a decade at least and, if you take the voting or drinking age as a marker, for nearly two. In such an extended period, an awful lot happens, both physically and psychologically.

It is fascinating to think about. Our brains and bodies are exquisitely designed to depend on one another. We are biologically designed to seek our mother from the moment of birth. Once we emerge into the outside world, we instantly look for her. When we find her, we have an urge to be close to her, to be fed by her, and to gaze into her eyes. I remember being so impressed by the elegance of this design when I was studying human attachment in school. I was captivated by the fact that the distance that a newborn baby can see is about twelve inches, which is essentially the distance necessary to see the face of the one who is holding the newborn.

Newborn babies prefer to look at faces more than anything else in the world. As human beings, we latch on both to feed from and to bond to another person. We want to take in the milk that Mother gives, but we want to take in the love, security, and beauty that she offers as well. Within a few days after we are born, we also know how to imitate another person. We can smile when she smiles, frown when she frowns, and, with time, coo when she coos and giggle when she giggles. We are oriented, both biologically and psychologically, to find another human being and shape ourselves in his or her likeness.

Even though this dependency orientation is so basic to our makeup, the process of becoming securely attached isn't so easy. While most babies have a strong innate potential to do so, it still takes work and effort. Consider breastfeeding as an analogy. There is a reason why mothers so often give up on breastfeeding and why lactation counselors have jobs. Both mother and baby have to learn and work to get connected. The same effortful work is needed to get connected in a psychological feeding relationship as well.

Psychoanalysts have given a lot of thought to the paradoxical reality that depending on someone can be so difficult when it seems, at the same time, to be so natural. Melanie Klein, Donald

Meltzer, Donald Winnicott, John Bowlby, Margaret Mahler, and Erik Erikson are among the great pioneers of this kind of research. Each, in their own way, observed that the process of becoming "properly dependent" is one of the most challenging and important foundational experiences of our lives.

I use the term "properly dependent" for a reason. As I discussed earlier, people tend to think that being dependent is a *bad* thing. We associate it with being needy, helpless, and vulnerable—and so we are repulsed by the mere thought of it. In our capitalistic society where the image of rugged American individualism is prized, there's a very contemptuous view of people who supposedly don't take care of themselves, who are perceived as not being self-sufficient. We call them takers, moochers, and freeloaders. We idealize independence and expect people to fend for themselves.

In my opinion, there is a time for such independence in one's development, but it can be a disaster if it happens too early, when you don't yet know what the heck you're doing. Proper dependency is the good and wholesome process of turning to someone else to take care of you, for a time, so that you can ultimately learn how to take care of yourself. In other words, you've got to learn how to do it before you can actually do it.

Now it's true that many emotional problems stem from being *too* dependent. How many parents have struggled with a child who was stuck to their side like glue, too frightened to go off to kindergarten or summer camp or college or life? How many children have struggled with parents who kept them too close, frightened to send them out into the world with their blessing? How many social workers have struggled with a client who is more capable than they claim to be? Being overly dependent is a serious problem.

Many people, however, find themselves at the opposite end of the spectrum, having been launched into life prematurely, without a secure or solid foundation for independence. These are the "parentified" children, the latchkey kids who didn't really have anyone reliable to depend on and had to figure things out for themselves. Some had parents who were so needy that the tables were turned; the parents depended on the children rather than the other way around. Children in families where there is addiction, poverty, violence, serious chronic illness, and/or divorce know something about these dynamics. In such situations, children miss out on the chance to really be children and, in turn, to develop independence in a healthy way and at the right time.

Proper dependency requires the presence of a capable parent upon whom a little one can rely. But it also requires the capable parent to encourage the little one to become more his own separate person, slowly over time. A capable parent is sensitive to the back-and-forth movement that children have and need to have in relationship with them. A capable mother provides what Margaret Mahler called "safe anchorage," a reliable home base from which the child can explore and to which he can return for emotional nourishment, comfort, and guidance.

In the very beginning, the process of developing a mind of one's own starts in a state of merger between baby and mother, what Margaret Mahler called "normal symbiosis" and Donald Winnicott called "undifferentiated unity." This is that early, early period when baby and mother have no clear sense of where one starts and the other begins. As normal development unfolds, a properly dependent relationship begins to emerge in which there is more separateness, that is, space for the baby to be connected to the mother but also to be distinct from her. This dynamic balance requires a lot of effort, particularly on the part of the mother, who must develop a sense of when to hold the baby close and when to let him go. This is the sweet spot of proper dependency. If you have experience raising or teaching or guiding little ones, you know how critical this balance can be.

If we extend this description of proper dependency in childhood to the relationship that we have with parental figures later in life, we can see how important it is to establish a relationship in which depending on an instructor, therapist, or other guide is used for the sake of development. Dependency is a good thing when its purpose is continued growth. In fact, it is positive and absolutely necessary for development. A relationship in which real feeding, nourishing, and guiding take place is the wellspring from which a healthy sense of self can develop.

A relationship in which real feeding, nourishing, and guiding take place is the wellspring from which a healthy sense of self can develop.

In my clinical work, I have come to discover that one of the reasons why psychoanalytic treatment typically lasts such a long time is because it is so difficult to establish this kind of proper dependency, or what we Kleinian analysts might call a proper feeding relationship. Believe it or not, patients fight getting themselves into the position of being dependent on the analyst.

Unable to stomach the reality that the analyst has what they need, many patients turn away out of envy. This happens so commonly that any analyst worth his or her salt has come both to accept it and expect it.

At first, patients have great difficulty listening to what their analyst has to say, ignoring it, dismissing it, arguing over it, or twisting it all around. In contrast, some patients put their analyst so high on a pedestal that they too readily agree with everything rather than try to think for themselves. In either case, the outcome is the same: no growth. Helping a patient find that sweet spot of being connected but separate is a formidable task in analysis. It means helping them move out of a more comfortable position of overdependency on the one hand or self-sufficiency on the other, into a position of proper dependency. Sometimes it can take years of analysis until a patient truly becomes a patient—if by a patient we mean someone who actually can take in what the analyst has to offer.

Because this dynamic is not commonly understood, it is very tempting to make fun of people, including certain celebrities, who have been in analysis for decades. From the outside, it is easy to think that analysis takes so long because one or both parties are resistant to ending it. But I think it is just as likely that analysis lasts so long because there is such resistance to properly beginning it.

Once established in life or analysis, the period of proper dependency is not a static state that is left behind. It is at once the foundation upon which our independence is built and the safe anchorage to which we return, over and over again, in a slow journey toward increasing independence. In other words, independence grows out of proper dependency and is also sustained by it.

RIPENING TO OBEDIENCE

Now if you cringe at the mention of the word *dependence*, you will probably start hyperventilating when I mention the word *obedience*. Let's face it, obedience, too, has a bad name in American society today. It has connotations of loss of freedom, mind control, and even cultlike dependence. We worry about people who are too obedient, that they are vulnerable to others abusing them or taking advantage of them.

Where once obedience was understood as the proper place of children in relationship to their parents, it went too far—too far into excessive strictness that didn't give children the space they needed to grow minds of their own. The same is true in certain governments where insistence on obedience to authority strips individuals of their right to think, to choose, and to disagree.

As a result, there has been a shift away from obedience toward a "child-centered" approach to learning that lets little ones direct more of the process. We can see that shift in some modern child-rearing practices and educational systems. Such a shift encourages creativity, curiosity, and personal responsibility. In moderation, this is an important correction to an overly rigid style of parenting and teaching. But if the pendulum swings too far, it is easy to see how chaos can ensue. We need to strike a balance. For me, obedience is the center point of this dynamic process, a fulcrum that balances proper dependence on the one side and inspired independence on the other.

Obedience, from a psychological viewpoint, describes the relationship between a child and a parent or between a student and a teacher or a patient and an analyst in which learning takes place. In order to learn, the student must put himself in a proper position vis-à-vis his teacher. He must sit on his bottom, as his kindergarten teacher might say. He must come to know his place in the pack and show deference to the authority of the master. If a student can develop the humility and good sense to do so, he may learn quite a lot.

An obedient relationship helps a child to become disciplined, both in his behavior and in his mind. An obedient child listens. An obedient child takes in the wise direction of his parents. An obedient child puts that direction into practice. And this he must do in order to develop a mind of his own.

This healthy kind of obedience relies on the child having a positive identification with his parental figures. A positive identification means that the child looks up to his parents and teachers, admires them, and wants to become like them. It may seem odd that I would say that a child must become like his parents in order to develop a mind of his own, but I think it is true. When we dress up in Mother's shoes, drive a toy car pretending to be like Dad, or take on the role of teacher when playing school, we are experimenting with what it would be like to be a grown-up.

When I was a teenager immersed in the evangelical Christian culture, there was an interesting method for teaching us how to make decisions in a mature, virtuous way. We were to ask ourselves an orienting question: What would Jesus do? If we could learn to think like Jesus thought and behave like Jesus did, then we would be on the right track to becoming a better person. Jesus, of course, represents the human ideal. People would wear buttons that read "WWJD?" to remind themselves and one another to be guided by Jesus and his way.

While that experience seems a million miles away to me now, there is something in it of lasting importance for me. I believe that it is essential to find someone whose wisdom you trust and whose way of living you admire—to walk in his or her footsteps and to learn of his or her ways. For example, while working on my own psychological development, I often asked myself, "What would my therapist do?" or "What would my therapist say?" My patients have told me that they ask such questions of themselves, too. This is an important step in developing a mind of your own, paving the way so that you can begin to ask yourself, "What would *I* do or say?"

As you can see, healthy obedience is rooted in respect and admiration of the parents' (or parental figures') skill, experience, and wisdom. There are many examples in religion, literature, and other great stories that bring this dynamic to life. One of my favorites is from the film *The Karate Kid*. It is a classic example of proper dependence ripening to obedience on its way to inspired independence.

The film depicts the teacher-student relationship between the karate master, Kesuke Miyagi, and his new student, Daniel LaRusso. If you've seen the film, you know that Mr. Miyagi is teaching Daniel not only about martial arts but about life itself. A fatherless child, Daniel is in great need of an adopted parental figure that he can look up to and from whom he can learn. He needs to learn to protect himself, both physically and psychologically.

Mr. Miyagi has agreed to teach Daniel karate and, in the process, establishes obedience as the central dynamic of their relationship. They make a pact in which Mr. Miyagi promises to teach and Daniel promises to learn, no questions asked. Then Mr. Miyagi tells Daniel to wash and wax all the cars in the lot. At first Daniel balks at the idea, but then he reluctantly obeys. The daylight wanes as Daniel continues to wax the cars, not understanding the purpose of the exercise but willing to do it because he trusts his master. Such a scene may help us rethink our usual disdain for the idea of a parent telling a child to do something "because I say so."

That is Mr. Miyagi's way and, early on, it is the way of all great masters. Because they know they have something important to give, they expect obedience from their pupils; it is a built-in requirement from the get-go. If you wish to learn, you must make the deal. Do what the master says, no questions. When that kind of contract can be made, real learning has a chance.

"Wax on, wax off," Mr. Miyagi says to Daniel. "Feel the force," Obi-Wan Kenobi tells Jedi knight-in-training Luke Skywalker. "Practice your scales," my trumpet teacher used to tell me. "Abandon memory and desire," psychoanalyst Wilfred Bion urged young analysts-in-training, just as the Buddha advised seekers centuries before. And in the process, these masters all reminded us to breathe.

Perhaps you see how obedience that emerges out of proper dependence has built-in safeguards against misuse and abuse. Such obedience is not mindless or cruel, for it is a two-way street characterized by love, gratitude, and good judgment. In this model, children obey their parents because their parents prove to them that they are worthy of their trust. They show, over and over again, that they are reliable, helpful, and devoted to their child's well-being. The child who can ripen into an obedient relationship with such parents has developed a sense that the parents' purpose is not to *control* him but to *teach* him.

INSPIRED INDEPENDENCE

Through ripening obedience, we learn the scales, study the forms, and practice the fundamentals. We prepare ourselves to step up, speak up, get up, and get going. We get ready for our vision quest. We take our exams, our bar or bat mitzvahs, our confirmations, our graduations. Once we show that we have mastered the basics of our master's technique, we must go out on our own to make our way in the world.

At these critical junctures between obedience and inspired independence, we are very fortunate if we have parents who have not only equipped us for the future but who encourage and bless us to move on without them. This is very difficult for some parents who are anxious to protect their children from the dangers of the world. But it is a gift to children if their parents can nudge them from the nest, for it is the only way that children can develop their own wings.

For parents, this process of letting go culminates in an external change that springs from a deep and hard-earned internal change. In order to push their child out of the nest, parents must push *themselves* in the process. They must encourage *themselves* to have faith that the basics that they have passed along to the child will be enough. They must reassure *themselves* that they have given their child enough of a start, enough of a foundation, enough to work with. From their child's infancy through adulthood, parents will encounter moments when they must challenge themselves to inspire their child's independence over and over again. In order to send them off to kindergarten or the freshman dormitory, to summer camp or boot camp, to the altar or the halfway house, parents must work hard to grow, too.

To become a capable parent, one must develop a sense of the ebb and flow of dependence and independence that is a natural part of a child's evolution. Capable parents work hard to discern what is needed at any given moment. Sometimes this means drawing a child close for reasons of safety or to promote discipline. Sometimes it means frustrating them, pushing them, and challenging them to go out on their own. This is not the kind of sense that can be learned from a book; it can only be learned through experience. In other words, the music of parenting requires more than good technique; it requires what jazz musicians call *feel*.

In order to become more independent, children must respond in kind. They must learn both to obey and to take the freedom that is given to them—and sometimes even take a bit of freedom when it is not given to them. Sometimes a child reaches forward with his parents' blessing and sometimes he must do it in rebellion. Both methods are necessary and inevitable aspects of leaving home if he is to make his own way.

Capable parents are also responsive to this struggle in the child. They tolerate the fussing, the rebelliousness, the pain of failure and disappointment, as well as the need for comfort and reassurance. They make room for the child to gather more and more experience as he works toward building a sense of his own competence.

In this long process, there are painful feelings that everyone must weather. As the child grows in feelings of competence, he will turn toward challenges and thus away from help. He will rebel, reject, and show contempt toward his parents. That hurts. But it is necessary in order for him to overcome his deep attachment to them. He must break the very bond that supports him. And, paradoxically, the parents must suffer it in order to keep the bond strong.

Inevitably, the child will reach beyond his capacities and fail, returning to the comfort and help of his parents who are waiting in the wings. With his confidence restored, out he goes again to try his newfound capacities in the world; he learns new lessons, succeeds, fails, and returns to home base once again. This is how little ones grow. Wash, rinse, repeat.

No matter how mature or successful we become, the child within always will need mentors and friends who'll see us through.

This dynamic process of trying, succeeding, failing, and trying again is the only way to develop lasting confidence in ourselves. We learn through experience that we can both succeed and recover from failure. We also learn to be humble and so develop a view of ourselves as limited creatures that will always need the help and support of others. No matter how mature or successful we become, the child within always will need mentors and friends who'll see us through.

What I have described so far is a kind of ideal process of separation, painful and challenging though it may be. I also want to make note of a kind of false process of independence that is common yet perhaps not commonly understood. True independence involves taking in the good of what our parents give us and taking it to the next step. False independence involves rejecting what our parents have given us entirely and pretending that we can make a good life for ourselves without it.

Independence that is based in rejection of our parents and their ways is not really independence at all. All of our so-called independent choices become an unconscious reaction to them. Rather than freeing ourselves from our parents, we become bound to them in hatred.

It is common for children, at certain points along the way, to reject their parents' values in their totality. How many times have you heard young people say that they want to be *nothing* like their parents? They reject their parents' religion, their politics, their wisdom, their dress, their culture, and their way of speaking. But when we reject our parents entirely—when we throw out the baby with the bathwater, so to speak—we are not thinking in an independent, mature way. We are being as small-minded, judgmental, and rigid as we believe them to be.

When, instead, we are able to take in, think about, and use what our parents give to us, when we let them mean something good to us, then we become independent in a proper way. The analogy of an alimentary tract is apt here. When we can chew on the food for thought that our parents give to us, when we can swallow it, digest what is nourishing, and eliminate the waste, then we have the chance to grow in the best and most proper sense.

I have experienced this process very clearly with my parents' religious faith, among other things. My sister describes our upbringing by saying that we were "hothouse Christians." What she means is that we were brought up in an intense religious environment, in which belief in God and following Jesus' way were central to our family culture. While my sister and I have traveled different paths in relationship to the faith of our parents, we have both been able to leave it and then later return to it on our own terms.

A lot of people raised in the Christian church are very critical of it, become disillusioned by organized religion, or have trouble believing some of the core theologies of the church, such as the virgin birth, the bodily resurrection of Jesus, or the inerrancy of Scripture. It is easy to reject religion entirely, viewing it, at its worst, as a manipulative way to control people. I bristle at the idea that we are supposed to take the Bible at face value and literally believe what it says just because it says it. I cringe when the message from the pulpit is that good Christians are to have unquestioning faith. That kind of faith is not for me, either.

But I have come to discover that there is a way to honor the faith of my upbringing, to be inspired by its values, and to do something good with them. If there is room for thinking, questioning, and doubt, then there is room for me. If I don't have to accept every bit as the truth with a capital T, then I become hopeful that there is room for dependence, obedience, and independence, all in good measure. You don't have to throw out the baby with the manger. For me, for now, I've decided that I'm good just with the baby—I'm good with the core values that Jesus taught and the way in which he embodied them. As the old hymn goes, "You can have all this world, just give me Jesus."

In contrast to false independence that rejects the parents, true and inspired independence involves taking in all that our parents give us—the good, the bad, whatever it may be—and making it our own. The best faith is a faith that we inherit and then refine in the fire of our own experience. The best improvisation is an embellished expression of the fundamentals. The frontier discoveries of science are creative elaborations of what was already known. Brilliant artists always create work that, in one way or another, bears the imprint of the master. This is what it means to evolve into inspired independence. What our parents have placed within us comes out, but in our own way and on our own terms.

In her autobiography, Helen Keller wrote about her relationship with her teacher, Anne Sullivan, in a way that poignantly captures this dynamic. She wrote:

> At the beginning I was only a little mass of possibilities. It was my teacher who unfolded and developed them. When she came, everything about me breathed of love and joy and was full of meaning. She has never since let pass an opportunity to point out the beauty that is in everything, nor has she ceased trying in thought and action and example to make my life sweet and useful . . . . My teacher is so near me that I scarcely think of myself apart from her. How much of my delight in all beautiful things is innate, and how much is due to her influence, I can never tell. I feel that her being is inseparable from my own, and that the footsteps of my life are in hers. All the best of me belongs to her—there is not a talent, or an aspiration or a joy in me that has not been awakened by her loving touch.[18]

This description of the connection between student and teacher—just like the intimate bond between child and parent—is about as good as it gets. Even for me, as a writer and psychoanalyst, I find that it is hard to know if I have ever had an original thought. I believe that every word I write and every insight I have to offer are developments of gifts that others have given to me. I am blessed to have been given good gifts from so many people, and I have had the discipline to take them in, appreciate them, be strengthened by them, and make them my own.

In this way, my parents and teachers live on inside me. They have become my inner voice. They are my mature internal parents. While I may grow separate from them, disagree with them, and even reach beyond them as I develop a mind of my own, they are always the source of my inspiration. I had this idea in mind when I read the following passage from Helen Keller's autobiography at my mother's funeral. I also had it in mind when I wrote the dedication for this book, "In memory of my mother from whom all blessings flow. All the best of me belongs to her. There is not a talent or an aspiration or a joy in me that has not been awakened by her loving touch."[19]

CHAPTER ELEVEN

IT'S ALWAYS BROKEN, SO WE ALWAYS HAVE TO FIX IT

On Love, Guilt, and Reparation

THE JOURNEY TOWARD MATURITY INVOLVES developing a mind of one's own. In this all-important process, we undergo radical changes in our view of the world and of ourselves. We shed our idealizations. We lose our innocence. We realize how complex life really is. We learn to take the good with the bad. We come to understand that real relationships require hard work and struggle. We discover that the things that matter the most don't come easily.

When I was in the first year of my psychoanalytic training, one of my teachers posed a basic question to our class. He asked, "What is Melanie Klein's model of the mind all about?" We were newbies at the time, struggling to wrap our heads around what seemed to be an incredibly complex set of theories. We responded tentatively, wondering if the answer had something to do with the unconscious inner world, or projection, or transference, or some other fancy psychoanalytic idea. Needless to say, we were stunned when he said that her model comes down to one thing. "Love," he said. "It's all about love."

So let us turn to what matters most.

Melanie Klein was very interested in understanding the human mind, but not only from the perspective of her research and clinical work as a psychoanalyst. It is well known that her work was also driven by her desire to better understand herself, trying as she was to understand her personal struggles with depression and the complicated relationships in her own life. She was particularly passionate about making sense of the process by which people learn to love one another—first as infants with our mothers and then, in time, with our fathers, siblings, friends, and children, and in lifelong partnerships such as marriage. She wrote a beautiful paper about these ideas, called "Love, Guilt, and Reparation."[20] It is essentially the story of how we learn to love one another in a real, Velveteen Rabbit kind of way.

Klein began with the idea that relationships are so difficult because we are innately so mistrustful. We are afraid that others will either harm us or leave us, and these are distressing expectations that we must work to overcome. The only way to overcome them is by allowing ourselves to have experiences with others that reassure us that our fear-based beliefs are not true, or at least not *entirely* true. But this does not come easily to us because, at some deep level, we feel that getting intimately involved with another person is dangerous. So we've got to jump in, even when we're scared. There's no other way around it. We've got to take the leap of faith so we can acquire positive experiences that challenge the validity of our doubts and fears. Only then can we believe that love is even possible.

Klein studied this jumping-in process to see what was involved. She found that in order to take the plunge, we must conjure up an image of other people as extraordinarily good and so perfectly loving that they would never hurt us. If we remember our first crush, we know just what she was talking about. By idealizing the other person, we disarm our fear about the risk that is involved. This allows us to jump in, give the relationship a try, and test whether or not our mistrust is warranted.

Such idealization is necessary at first but, of course, never lasts. Through experience, we realize that people are usually not as bad as we imagine them to be. But we also realize that they are not so ideal either—and neither are we—and that hurt, disappointment, and loss are inevitable aspects of even the most decent, loving relationships.

Nevertheless, it is good to allow ourselves to have these real experiences. By so doing, we give ourselves a chance to develop the capacity to bear the pains of hurt and loss, and to discover that love is not ruined or diminished by them. One of Klein's most important discoveries—perhaps not unique to her, but illuminated greatly by her—is that our effort to repair the brokenness in our relationships is actually what makes them stronger. Perfection is fragile and fleeting; real relationships are sturdy and enduring.

In this chapter, we're going to explore how we move through our fears, idealizations, and disappointments, and so learn to love. The Garden of Eden story captures this process in a vivid way, and I'm going to use it as a vehicle for thinking about living and loving in the face of brokenness. But I want to see if we can approach the story from a different perspective, or even from a few different perspectives, because I think the usual literal interpretation is only one aspect of the story's wisdom. Perhaps if we take a closer look, we'll learn a few more things about ourselves.

Nearly every religious tradition has a Garden of Eden story, and it can be found in the mythology of ancient civilizations that were around long before the Jewish and Christian scriptures we have today. The story is an attempt to answer the question that people have asked since the beginning of time: Why is the world so broken?

In the Judeo-Christian version, the world was first conceived as an idyllic place in which there was no sickness or death. The earth provided all that was needed for sustenance and pleasure; man and woman lived with one another in peace and tranquility. It was a Golden Age without real suffering or grief. Innocence was cherished and ignorance was bliss.

As the story goes, everything was set up to remain perfect as long as man and woman—Adam and Eve—remained obedient to God. The story portrays them as the happy children of a supreme and loving parent. The world was meant to be both their playground and their paradise, as long as they honored one condition. One simple condition. They could have their pick of all the delicious fruit in the abundant garden, except for the fruit of one particular tree. They were not to eat the fruit of the tree of the knowledge of good and evil. For if they did, God said, they would surely die.

Seems doable, right? But, ah, the temptation! We know it so well. To hear the Serpent tell the tale, the tree of the knowledge of good and evil bore the most wonderful fruit in the whole garden. "Don't mind God's warning," he told them. That's just a stingy God protecting his own territory. No, if they ate of the tree of the knowledge of good and evil, they would not die as God had forewarned. Instead, their lives would become better, not worse. The Serpent tempted the humans with a promise as juicy as the fruit itself: If they ate of the tree's fruit, they would become gods themselves and never die.

It was an offer too good to refuse. To have it all, with no negative repercussions, that was the ticket, that was the *real* paradise. So Eve succumbed to the seduction of the Serpent and Adam yielded to his wife's wide-eyed enticement for him to join the party. Greed and envy won the day.

According to the story, a party did not ensue. Adam and Eve were not catapulted to the status of gods. While their act led to knowledge, it wasn't the delicious knowledge that the Serpent had promised. Instead, knowledge was experienced by the humans as self-consciousness, which came with a heavy dose of shame and fear. The Serpent promised that they would have more, but instead, even the peace of mind and harmony they had previously had was lost forever.

Indeed, God was so displeased upon finding out about their transgression that he cast them out of the Garden, separating them from all the good they once enjoyed in abundance. As if that weren't enough, God added suffering into the mix. Everything they would do from that point on—from childbirth to work to death—would be more arduous and painful.

If you take the story at face value—as if these events had *literally* happened, and for the reasons described—then you would take from it the idea that expulsion from the Garden is the end of an idyllic story and the beginning of a sad, painful one. You might even get the idea that suffering was never meant to be. The toil, pain, and profound sense of alienation that we experience are all a big mistake. The world wasn't supposed to be broken. It didn't have to be this way. And someone is to blame.

Most of us have this kind of view of the world. We believe that the world is a mess and that it shouldn't be this bad. Like Hägar the Horrible, we rage against the tides, lamenting the condition of this world and believing that it should be better than it is. We just can't accept that it is supposed to be this way.

Linked to this sense that the world is broken is a belief that someone, somewhere did something wrong to make it so. We want to blame someone, in the hope that this will make us feel better. The Devil made me do it. My wife made me do it. My parents didn't give me enough. I was set up; the temptation was too great. We profess our innocence: It's not my fault!

... how we think about the brokenness of the world has a lot to do with how we go about living in it.

Whether we come by such views through a particular religious tradition or simply by being human, these basic assumptions are pretty much universal. I want to shake things up a little and show you how we tend to take these assumptions to be facts when, actually, they are just points of view. I believe that it is important to question these points of view, because how we think about the brokenness of the world has a lot to do with how we go about living in it.

So let's view the story with the help of the wisdom of psychoanalysis. Let's keep in mind that this alternative approach is a point of view, too. But it just might lead to new understanding.

Whether we are searching for the fountain of youth, unconditional love, or a transcendental mountaintop experience, we human beings seem to have an innate longing to return to a lost ideal, a protected, blissful state. Some call it the Garden of Eden. Others call it Nirvana. Psychoanalysts call it the womb. In any case, it seems clear that we have a picture of a perfect place that we once inhabited, and then lost, and now we're trying to find again.

Klein believed this feeling of displacement from an ideal place is a common experience that can be traced back to very early events in life. In Klein's model, life begins with a fantasy that we once inhabited a perfect place in which we were always satisfied, safe, and loved. We didn't have a care in the world or the need to think, work, or struggle. She called that idyllic place the womb, the place where all our needs were met before we even knew we had them. There's a joke among Kleinian analysts that we all miss the time in our lives when we had twenty-four-hour "womb service." The kitchen of our mother's body never closed. We imagine that being in the womb was the most wonderful time of our lives, the Eden of our individual experience.

Klein observed in the play of young children that the experience of birth feels like being cast out of that perfect place, which is why we carry a sense of a lost paradise throughout our whole lives. Because of this early loss and similar losses that follow (especially weaning), she believed that our personalities are formed around a pervasive sense that something is always missing. We feel this as a persistent ache and an abiding sense of loss. The poet Rilke called it "the great homesickness we can never shake off." St. Augustine called it the "God-shaped hole" in the human soul. Klein called it "pining." We long for what is missing.

So the foundation of the human personality is this: Being alive, inevitably, brings an ever-present sense of loss and an ever-present pining for wholeness. We long for restoration, reconnection, and reconciliation. As I read it, that message is central to the Garden of Eden story.

Being alive also involves bearing the painful sense that things are not as they could or should be. It means living with the awareness that brokenness is always part of the human experience. That idea is also woven into the Eden story.

So much of life, then, becomes an effort to either avoid or cope with these basic psychological realities. Rather than accepting and facing them, we often fight against them instead. We imagine magical solutions. We conjure up a picture of a shallow heaven in which everything will be perfect—a no-more-tears-or-crying and the-streets-are-paved-with-gold kind of heaven. Or we strive for a kind of rigid perfection in this life, trying to transcend the human condition by becoming superhumans or supermartyrs or superzealots of one kind or another.

As I pointed out earlier, we also might try to return to Nirvana by inducing a high through alcohol or other drugs, sex, food, exercise, or other activities that produce excitement or bliss. We want to both numb the pain and enhance the pleasure. That's one of the reasons why addictions are so hard to break. They give us the illusion that there is a quick and easy way back to Eden.

We also pin our hopes on trying to find another person to fill the hole. We search for unconditional love, for an idealized romantic love, and for a sense of merged oneness with another person so that we do not have to feel alone. The idea that we could find another person to fill that hole is an appealing myth we would all like to believe. It goes back to the early Greeks who believed that we were each split in half and now wander through life searching for the lost half that would make us whole again.

In addition to this fundamental sense of loss and longing, there is another psychological aspect to the story. Human experience involves a set of feelings that are even more acutely painful: guilt and persecution. According to the Eden story and Klein's psychoanalytic model of the mind, we must contend with a belief that things are broken for a particular reason. We try to make sense of the brokenness of the world by way of the fantasy that somebody did something wrong and needs to be punished for it.

It's easy to relate to this idea. During the time we were little kids, we worried about getting in trouble, and we carry that worry into adult life, too. It keeps some of us awake at night, gives others migraine headaches, and drives others to drink. Sometimes we know we are guilty and expect to be punished. Other times we expect people in authority to be unfairly harsh and quick to lay blame. The principal or boss asks you to come to his office. Your father says he needs to talk to you about something. The doctor's office calls. You see a police car in your rearview mirror. Your heart rate quickens; you feel like you've been caught doing something wrong. This is what guilt and persecution feel like. God's voice echoes in the Garden, "Adam, what have you done?"

Klein observed that these feelings and fantasies are present from the earliest days of life. The baby's experience of birth feels not only like a loss, but also like a persecution. Klein carefully traced the feelings of little ones in early childhood back to birth, deducing that being born feels like being bombarded by something bad from the outside. It makes sense. Our first exposure to the world feels painful: The air is cold, the lights are bright, and the doctor's gentle slap hurts. We must work to breathe; we must work to find our mother. At the moment of birth, suddenly, we are conscious of our separateness and we are flooded with anxiety. Stimulation from the outside world attacks our peace of mind; our sense of comfort has been radically disturbed. We are naked and vulnerable in a dangerous world.

As I observe myself, my patients, and many people whom I have come to know well, I can see what Klein was talking about. Indeed, we seem to have a preconception that the world was once perfect and a conviction that it should still be that way. We idealize that blissful state with its allure of effortlessness, mindlessness, and unconditional love. As a result, it is hard to accept the world outside of the womb for the reality it is. We believe everything should be easy; we don't believe life should be so darn complicated, never mind so darn painful. And so we experience the pressures of life as unnecessary and unfair. We feel persecuted by them.

Since we are psychological creatures, not just biological ones, we try to make sense of these feelings. Psychological creatures ask why. Why is this happening to me? What accounts for the shift from good to bad, from pleasure to pain, from bliss to suffering? Why am I on the outside now, rather than the inside? We might say that the Garden of Eden story is a description of how the newborn answers these questions. Before we have the cognitive capacity to even conceive of such a sophisticated concept as guilt, we have a visceral sense of it. We have a sense that we are on the outside now because somebody did something wrong.

Our first line of defense is to blame ourselves. If we feel bad, we imagine we must be bad. If we feel guilty, we imagine we must be guilty. And the truth is that often we are. After all, we know more than anyone else the greed and hatred that are in our hearts and minds. If we are truly honest with ourselves, we know that we are prone to disobedience, rebelliousness, greed, and envy. We know our hostile thoughts and feelings. And even if we don't act on them, we feel bad because we have them.

Ironically, we have tried to maintain an idealized belief about the innocence of babies. But, really, if you've ever met a baby (or ever been a baby), you know better. If you read the Garden of Eden story with a close eye, you see that Adam and Eve were never all that innocent either.

But our guilt feelings are complicated. Sometimes we feel guilty when we haven't actually done anything wrong. We fall on our swords just to tidy up complicated psychological realities. Maybe we are afraid of calling a spade a spade. Maybe we don't want to blame someone we love. Maybe we are too obedient and reluctant to defend ourselves. I know these feelings well. In fact, I am so guilt-prone that I consider myself an expert on the topic. As a case in point, I joke with my husband that our lives would go so much better if we just blamed me for all of our problems! I'm joking, of course.

But if we carry forward this "somebody is to blame" mind-set, we must remember there are two sides to every story. Children are not the only guilty ones. There are parents and bosses and principals and cops and gods that share some of the blame, too. Those in authority can set up no-win situations. They can be quick to judge and slow to understand. They can be envious and greedy themselves, holding others back because they get so much satisfaction or comfort from being in charge. They may want others to grow in knowledge and understanding of the world, but they may also feel quite threatened by it. If you look carefully, that theme can also be detected in the story of Adam and Eve.

So, as we dig deeper and deeper into the human story, we discover these two great psychological themes. Psychological life inescapably involves a sense of loss and longing and a sense of guilt and persecution. Even the most optimistic personality feels the ache of depression, disappointment, and anxiety that is part of the human condition. For me, psychological growth comes down to sorting out these dynamics and finding a way to manage them well.

———

I hope to have shown how the Garden of Eden story and Klein's model of the mind shed a similar light on our core psychological struggles. But I'm going to mix it up even more. You see, Klein didn't just take the human story at face value. She didn't believe that our views are entirely accurate. To the mix, she added an essential bit that makes a world of difference. She made it more explicit that this particular view of the human story is a *fantasy*. She didn't believe that the world was supposed to be perfect and is now broken. She didn't believe that the brokenness of the world was someone's fault. She didn't believe that this view of life was a view of reality. She believed it is how the world looks from the point of view of the baby.

So what happens if we change our perspective accordingly? What happens if we view the story—the Garden of Eden story, the human story—not as a factual account of why the world is so broken, but as a story about the journey from the dependency of infancy to the obedience of childhood, ripening into the inspired independence of adulthood? What if it is really a coming-of-age story about how we learned to think about a complex world in which contrary and conflicting realities live side by side: good and bad, love and hate, free will and obedience, as well as the angels and demons of our human nature? What if the story is really about learning to love, with all the conditions, pain, and separateness that are part of being human? In other words, *What if Adam and Eve were supposed to eat the apple?*

If we changed our perspective, we'd have to take new starting points. One new starting point would be that the world was broken from the beginning. By broken I mean that life was never in perfect balance or harmony, nor was it ever meant to be. Perfection and bliss are illusions. Innocence is a myth. Life always has and always will involve conflict, work, struggle, and death. These are natural and value-neutral aspects of life. Brokenness isn't anyone's fault. It isn't a punishment. It just is.

> *Life always has and always will involve conflict, work, struggle, and death. These are natural and value-neutral aspects of life.*

Buddhists are ahead of the rest of us in accepting this truth. As mentioned earlier, Buddha understood that the nature of life is suffering. He didn't mean that life is a dark hole without happiness or satisfaction. He meant that life is imperfect and impermanent. Just as Adam and Eve became enlightened, so Buddha himself came to understand that pain, sickness, aging, and death are unavoidable aspects of life. So, too, are emotional pains such as disappointment, anxiety, depression, and loneliness. But Buddha didn't blame anyone for it. He simply encouraged us to accept suffering as one of the basic truths of human existence, the starting point of life's noble path.

If we take imperfection and impermanence as our starting points, we save ourselves a lot of unnecessary suffering. No more raging at the tides. We are more able to let the tides do what they do—come and go as they please.

There are stories in many cultures about the importance of keeping in mind the inevitable reality of human imperfections. Deliberate mistakes are said to be woven into rugs (the Persian Flaw), or blankets (the Navajo Nick), or quilts (the Amish Humility Block). By intentionally embedding these flaws into their creative work, the artists keep in mind our imperfection as human beings. Such discipline is designed to keep our spirits humble and our feet firmly planted in the real world. Some experts dismiss these stories as myths rather than actual practices, saying that one does not need to *deliberately* make mistakes in such works of art, as mistakes are unavoidable. In either case, the point is clear: There is no such thing as perfection in this world of ours.

The second new starting point would be that human beings are designed to be highly emotional creatures. We do not come into this world as blank slates. There is no such thing as a tabula rasa. We are not simpletons, innocent children, or robots. We are three-dimensional. We are psychologically rich beings. To be alive means to have a whole range of feelings and impulses: the good, the bad, and the ugly. Aggression, love, and the ability to think and choose are all part of the way we are meant to be. The story is reconceived as a description of a state of being rather than the diagnosis of a problem. We are not broken because something went wrong. We are broken because that is what it means to be human.

Envy, greed, and disobedience were there from the beginning, inevitably and by design. We wouldn't be human without them. Curiosity and ambition could not have vitality without them. There is a thin line between our ill-fated striving for superiority and our constructive aspirations. The desire for the knowledge of good and evil may be an attempt to overthrow our parents, but it is, at the same time and on another level, an effort to develop a true morality for ourselves. How can we be faulted for such striving? It is part and parcel of the developmental process of becoming adults in our own right, which is actually what our parents and our gods say they want from us in the first place.

There is a corollary to the idea that we are complex, emotional creatures—namely, that our parents are, too. So is God, if you believe in one and you're paying attention. As we discussed in the last chapter, parents are human beings, too. They struggle with the very same feelings and impulses as their children. Every parent is also a child. Envy, greed, and disobedience are everyone's lot, just as guilt, love, and the desire to do the right thing are central to our human nature. It is just the way things are.

Abraham Heschel, the influential Jewish philosopher, believed that God is a complex emotional being. Heschel coined a term to describe God's three-dimensional nature. He called it "the divine pathos," portraying the God of Israel as an emotional being, a concerned and feeling God.[21] Heschel's God is not Aristotle's "unmoved mover" but the "most moved mover" of the Bible, including the Garden of Eden story. For Heschel, God set up the world in a particular way, in such a way that people would be capable of having a real relationship with him. For Heschel, God *wants* to have a real relationship with us, one that we choose to have with him. Even more, for Heschel, God *needs* to have a relationship with us in order to exist. The complex nature of our relationship with God is what makes it meaningful for us and for God. A beautiful idea.

Finally, we have the opportunity to take as a new starting point the idea that we are fundamentally alone, and that our separation from others is the nature of things and what makes us unique individuals. Forgive me if I am overly influenced by my Western, individualistic worldview, but I think there is something valuable to be learned here. We are not fused beings split apart from one another, searching for our lost selves. We are separate selves—individuals—looking to find connection with others. This may be a subtle distinction, but it is an important one. It takes the bite out of the reality of our aloneness. It helps us appreciate the connections we have with one another, seeing them as blessings rather than entitlements. It helps us accept the reality that relationships take work. Such work is not a punishment. Again, it is just the way things are.

In his marvelous little book *Letters to a Young Poet*, Rainer Maria Rilke put it this way: "Ultimately, and precisely in the deepest and most important matters, we are unspeakably alone; and many things must happen, many things must go right, a whole constellation of events must be fulfilled, for one human being to successfully advise or help another."[22] Rilke was trying to help his young friend understand that the poet must find his way on his own and that moments of connection with another are rare treasures. If we can see connection with others in this light—as something precious, unexpected, and undeserved—then we may find ourselves to be less persecuted and more accepting of the aloneness that is a natural part of the human condition. We may also be less likely to take our relationships for granted.

The Garden of Eden story captures this truth in God's own words: "It is not good for Man to be alone" (Genesis 2:18). It's true. It doesn't feel good to be alone. We don't like it. But it is the fundamental state of things. And if we do things right, if we really work at it, we will have moments of connection with one another that we can cherish as the blessings that they are.

The framework has now been laid to explore the dynamic of love more directly. You might not have imagined that the framework of mature love would involve brokenness, guilt, separateness, and even aloneness. At first, neither did I. But everything we have said so far about the nature of the human condition applies to the nature of love.

Usually, when we think of love, we picture a connection with another that is easy, effortless, and bathed in good feelings. We are infatuated with the idea of unconditional love—a relationship in which we are loved just as we are, with no expectations or demands placed upon us. We long for a relationship in which we are loved no matter what we do. Our beloved is never disappointed in us, never asks anything of us, and is delighted to see us whenever we walk into a room.

By now you can see that these ideas amount to wishful thinking rather than reality. They are how we imagine a baby and a mother feel in one another's presence, but, if you've ever been there, you know those feelings last for about ten minutes, if you're lucky. Then the work begins. Even in the best of relationships, two separate people must work to come together. They must learn how to express themselves. They must learn how to read each other. They must learn how to bear the fact that they each have needs, and these needs are sometimes conflicting. They must learn to wait, to tolerate disappointment, to live up to the expectations of the other, to cooperate, to respect, and to be apart from each other. While there are moments of synergy and being at one, these are delightful exceptions to the rule. I hate to burst the bubble, but there is no such thing as unconditional love.

Mature love accepts the reality of the conditions. It understands that love is never ideal. It takes up the work required. It honors the fact of separateness. It respects the differences between individuals, and even appreciates them. When one feels "complete" in this kind of union, it has a different meaning. Rather than idealized love in which two come together as one, mature love brings two together as better than either one would be alone. I think that this kind of partnership is really what Eve meant to Adam, and Adam meant to Eve. Perhaps it is even what God meant to have with us, and what we are meant to have with God.

Kahlil Gibran captured this essential dynamic in a poem that is often shared at weddings,[23] including my own. He urged couples to allow for space in their togetherness. Just as the strings of a lute are alone, he noted, so they combine together to make beautiful music. So, too, the pillars of a temple must stand apart from one another in order to make a strong base. The Catholic theologian Henri Nouwen[24] also understood the fundamental importance of honoring separateness in our intimate relationships. He wrote that intimacy is a lot like dancing, where there needs to be a balance of aloneness and closeness in order for the two partners to move well together. Dancers must have enough distance between them so that they don't step on one another's toes but not so much distance that they will be out of sync. While the perfect balance of this relational dance seldom occurs, Nouwen believed that the honest search for such separate-togetherness is the mark of mature love.

Perhaps you can see more and more how real love is made strong in the gaps. Separateness has its advantages. The fact that there are differences between us means that you bring strengths to the relationship that I might not have, and vice versa. Our differences may complement one another, may challenge me to broaden my thinking, and may urge me to grow in an area of personal weakness. A passage in Proverbs 27:17 conveys this truth: "As iron sharpens iron, so one person sharpens another." Differences and friction propel us to growth.

It is difficult, however, to maintain this separate-but-connected way of relating with each other. It means you have to be in touch with the reality of your aloneness, which is painful. It means you have to be tolerant of the other's freedom to be his or her own person, which is maddening. I liken this separate-but-connected balance to the dynamic tension created when you hold two magnets right next to each other. There is a powerful pull for the magnets to attach to each other and fuse, just as there is a powerful pull for them to repel and disconnect. Mature love is the capacity to be in a dynamic relationship where connection and separateness exist side by side. It takes work to handle the tension in-between.

But there is much to gain from keeping this optimal balance in mind, even though it is always unfinished, always a work in progress. If we understand that love is an ongoing process of building a bridge over the gap of our separateness, we will be more forgiving of the fact that there is so much effort involved. One of my mentors likes to say that in marriage you have to earn your partner's love every day. That is an idea worth pondering. If you don't know about it, or if you refuse to accept it, it is easy to become resentful and frustrated. But if you can accept the reality that love takes work, you are likely to feel less persecuted by it.

Finally, we must draw the parallel between the brokenness that is elemental to the human condition and the brokenness that is elemental to human love. The experience of brokenness in love is very painful. The heartache that comes from lost love is perhaps the most painful experience of all. But we can take comfort in the fact that the pain is a direct expression of how much the love meant to us. The saying may be trite, but it is true: "It wouldn't hurt so much if it didn't mean so much."

Mature love—whether in marriage, family relationships, or friendships—is a dynamic, living experience. It is something you choose every day. It is something that is earned every day. It requires commitment to keep it working. It involves a daily process of overcoming the distance and honoring the separateness between us. It accepts the reality that we will hurt one another and be hurt by one another. It is the nature of being human. These pains cannot be avoided. We can only devote ourselves to do what we can do to weather them and to mend them.

So essentially, then, love is repair work. We tend to the hurts. We try to heal them. We express our concern. We take responsibility for our mistakes; we learn to say we're sorry. We try to make amends. We learn to forgive; we accept the forgiveness of another. As the monks do every day, we fall down and get up, fall down and get up again.

The sad truth is that all love ends. That is the reality, too. Sometimes a relationship can't withstand the work required. Sometimes it just was never meant to be. Sometimes it lasts for a season but not for a lifetime. But, in every case, time wields its power. Death comes to us all. And when it does, someone is almost always left behind. Then a different kind of mending must be done. We must grieve and we must do so alone. But if we have properly understood the nature of love, we retain ourselves—and this allows us to hold onto the memories of our love so that they can continue to strengthen us and ripen within us. In mature love, we can go on and carry our loved ones in our hearts and minds.

A few months ago, I was driving along in the car while listening to music. I was contemplating these ideas, percolating on this great trio of the mature psyche: love, guilt, and reparation. A song came on, a hymn I recognized from childhood. I promised myself I would hold onto the words of that hymn for this very passage, as they capture the message of this chapter beautifully: "Redeeming love has been my theme and shall be 'til I die, and shall be 'til I die." I love the pairing of words in the phrase *redeeming love*. The writer must have understood the deep truth that love and redemption are inseparable. As I say, it's always broken, so we always have to fix it.

CHAPTER TWELVE

LOVE IS THE NAME OF THE GAME

On Finding a Guiding Star

THIS BOOK ESSENTIALLY IS ABOUT dealing with reality—psychological reality, that is. It is a book about the life of the mind and how it works in reality, both on the inside and on the outside. My hope is that if you can better understand the nature of psychological reality, you will be better able to deal with it.

Students who are training to become psychotherapists often get this backward. From the earliest days of class, they want to learn psychotherapy technique, that is, what to do, what to say, and how to intervene to help their patients. While their hearts are in the right place, they put the cart before the horse; they want to start "fixing" people before they learn to understand them. They unwittingly try to bypass the necessary first step of studying and learning how the mind works. So I must caution them. First things first. You wouldn't put your car in the hands of a mechanic who doesn't understand how an engine works, would you? So don't go tinkering around in somebody's mind before you've studied the operator's manual.

Perhaps you've felt a similar impatience in reading these pages. Maybe you, too, have had to put the brakes on the urge to skip ahead to the how-to, application section. We all feel this pressure. I see it in my patients all the time. We barrel ahead without looking at or even asking for directions. We are so busy running around, trying to get things done, that we don't even realize we don't understand what we're trying to do. Staying with the car analogy, if we can slow ourselves down and develop an understanding of how the engine of our minds works, we can learn to take care of ourselves (keep up with the maintenance, take in the right fuel, make the necessary repairs) and even drive better (learn the rules of the road, follow directions, get where we want to go).

. . . while understanding is essential to creating a meaningful life, it is not an end in itself. Understanding is merely the blueprint for change.

So throughout this book, I have been working to reorient you—just like I work to reorient my students, my patients, and sometimes even myself. I must orient us to a different starting point, that of understanding. Once you understand how psychological reality works, the fixing will follow.

However, while understanding is essential to creating a meaningful life, it is not an end in itself. Understanding is merely the blueprint for change. The wisdom of this book—just like the wisdom of psychoanalysis—is not meant for the museum or the ivory tower or the philosophy books. It is meant to be used. It is meant to be applied to real life. It is meant to be put into practice so that we can function better. And by functioning better, I mean *feel* better, *do* better, and, if you're really ambitious, *be* better. A life that is understood well is a life meant to be lived well.

This leads us to a key question that we all must ask ourselves: What do you want out of your life? What does a life well lived look like to you?

It's easy to see that most people want to feel better in their lives. It's this desire that motivates people to go see a therapist in the first place, or to pick up and read a book like this. They want relief from distress. They long for their depression to be lifted, their anxiety to be quelled, or their grief to pass. When this relief comes, many people are ready to move on, to reenter their lives and go about living in pretty much the same way that they did before. Feeling better is an enormous relief. It's all they thought possible. For some, it is enough.

But others want more. Some people want to develop the skills and capacity to do better in their lives over the long term. They want to cope better and function better. They want to do better at work, in their relationships, and in their care for themselves. They want more than relief from their greatest anxieties; they want a better foundation for living. These are the folks who have the inner motivation to dig deeper and work harder at the home improvement project that is their life.

For people who invest in their personal growth in this way, there comes a point when they feel like they've gotten the hang of dealing with reality. They are in the groove, in the flow, and in the zone. In therapy, this point reveals itself when a patient feels like she has received from the treatment what she came for. She is satisfied. She feels more capable, more able to cope, more confident that she can carry the work of the treatment forward into the future on her own.

But then a new question arises: Does she want even more? At the beginning of treatment, she never imagined there was more. She just wanted to feel better. She never imagined that she could do as well as she is doing now. But as her life becomes more and more stable, she catches a glimpse of something even greater; not only a life that works, wonderful as that is, but a life that is deeper, more satisfying, and more meaningful. She must ask herself, "How deep do I want to go?" It is an important question, because a deep life is something of great value and something you really have to work for.

So this book is not just about how psychological things are and how they work; it is also about how to think about what you want out of life and how you want to go about living it. When we speak of wisdom, we enter into a world of meaning, of values, even of virtue. We come full circle. We must speak again about what we addressed in the first pages. We must speak about what we might want to make besides money, and what we might want to make of our lives.

I have found a longing in all of my patients for a way of thinking about life that helps orient them to living it better. They want to know how to know if they're doing well, if they're on the right track. They ask, "What do I look for? What do I aim for? What's the measure? What's the standard? What's the goal?" These are essential, important questions. Everybody needs a guiding star.

While I think most everyone wants to feel better, the desire to do better and to be better varies greatly from person to person.

People in my circle don't all agree on where they want to go, how far they want to go, or how deep they want to go. I am going to lay out for you the various options that are available—at least the healthy options that are available—and then you must decide for yourself which of these paths is right for you.

There are many useful guidelines for life that have been cast and recast since the beginning of time. You can find some of these in the oaths taken by physicians, judges, presidents, and youngsters in scouting troops. These guidelines are carved on monuments, inscribed on tablets, sewn into flags, and set to the tunes of music and poetry. "Do no harm." "Be prepared." "Love your neighbor as yourself." These are tried-and-true guiding stars. As Rabbi Hillel put it in the first century, "The rest is just commentary."

If you're looking for the kind of details that come with the commentary, you can't go wrong if you take as your guide the greatest hits album known as the Ten Commandments. If you're looking for a more contemporary and practical set of guidelines, you can't do much better than Robert Fulghum's book *All I Really Need to Know I Learned in Kindergarten.* For a well-researched, scholarly approach, I point you to Jonathan Haidt's *The Happiness Hypothesis.* Professor Haidt gets to the heart of it when he says that happiness is found through a combination of loving bonds with others, meaningful work, and a connection to something greater than oneself. That's some true wisdom right there.

In what follows I will share my own guiding principles I work over and work through every day with my patients in my clinical practice, as well as in the daily practice of my own life. They are my personal packaging of some timeless truths.

GUIDING STAR #1: *DO WHAT WORKS*

To the extent that successful psychological living is rooted in dealing well with reality, the principle of *do what works* is a pretty good entry-level guiding star. Like Occam's razor, it cuts through a lot of complexity and baloney, getting down to the basics. I like the simplicity of *do what works* because it orients us to dealing with reality as it is, rather than getting lost in fantasies about what might be or regrets about what could have been. It saves us from being held captive by the toddler-tantrum "I want what I want when I want it." It liberates us from the dead-end pursuit of "what-ifs" and "if-onlys." *Do what works* spares us from chasing after the wind.

The principles of daily living that undergird *do what works* vary from the practical to the virtuous. They involve unpretentious tenets like play by the rules. Work for a living. Be responsible. Show up and pay your bills on time. Listen. Think before you act. Eat less and exercise more. Be honest. Tell the truth. Own up to your mistakes. Make amends. Honor your commitments.

I think that it is useful to consider how these rudimentary principles apply to everyday life. Think about it. When we do what works, we engage in a cooperative relationship with others and with reality. When we move in concert with the framework that has been set up by society, there is elbow room. We are not burdened by calls from landlords, bill collectors, the IRS, or the doctor's office. We don't have to pay penalties for bounced checks, late payments, speeding tickets, or missed time on the job. When we do what is expected of us, we don't have to look over our shoulders all the time. We aren't plagued by guilt or wracked with anxiety. We don't need to defend ourselves, cover up our bad choices, or play the unending catch-up game. When we take care of our business, we are liberated from all the problems that inevitably arise when we don't.

In essence, the principle of *do what works* involves taking charge of your life in a grown-up way. To be effective, you must preside over your life. You sit at the head of your own table. You take the steering wheel of your life rather than giving it over to someone else. You establish yourself as the trustee, the supervisor, the manager, the CEO of your life. You decide that the buck stops with you; you arrange your inner psychological family so that the adult-you drives the car and the baby-you is strapped in the car seat where she safely belongs.

The guiding star of *do what works* makes sense to a lot of people. It is both practical and reasonable. For some, it is an extremely satisfying way to operate. For others, it is a solid foundation on which to build something more.

GUIDING STAR #2: *DO THE RIGHT THING*

Once you're in a proper relationship with reality—as in *do what works*—you are in a position to take your approach to life up a notch. You have a chance to up the ante by getting yourself into a proper relationship with others and with yourself, too. Here, the guiding star is also rather straightforward: *Do the right thing.*

Do the right thing is my version of what others call the rule of reciprocity or fairness. You begin to consider your life choices within the broader context of your relationships with others. You realize that your satisfaction in life is entwined with the world in which you live and the other people who live in it. At the very least, operating with a sense of fairness brings order and stability to our lives, helps us determine right from wrong, and is the basis of ethics and morality. But even beyond that, fairness helps us get along with other people by learning to share, to wait our turn, and to show some respect.

As a guiding star, *do the right thing* helps us overcome some base impulses that we all have, such as greed and envy. It cools the hot heels of impulses toward aggression, violence, and retaliation. With *do the right thing* as our guide, we are more likely to be safe and courteous drivers, to be slower to anger, and to give others the benefit of the doubt. Not only is this a way that works, it is a way that helps us feel better about others, as well as ourselves. *Do the right thing* is a further step toward real peace of mind.

Do the right thing means setting a high standard for ourselves. It is a kind of supercharged fairness that is quite different from the anemic, cynical views of fairness that some people try to pass off as the real deal. "Tit for tat" and "quid pro quo"—what the ancients called "talion law"—involve petty scorekeeping that keeps us stuck rather than moving forward. You-scratch-my-back-I'll-scratch-yours and an-eye-for-an-eye may technically qualify as fairness, but they don't take us very far.

It's easy to see that such a miserly approach to fairness may offer the appearance of evenhandedness but how, in practice, it devolves very quickly. It is limited because we are determining how we behave based on how someone behaves toward us. We're not in the driver's seat then. We're reacting in a mechanical way without real thought or judgment. We're looking to someone else to show us how to be. And that's not a guiding star. That's a crapshoot.

So when I think of reciprocity or fairness as an overarching principle, I have something more evolved in mind. That's why I like to call it *do the right thing*, which is more or less the same idea as the Golden Rule that we learned in kindergarten: Do unto others as you would have them do unto you. Not as they actually do unto you, but as you would want them to do unto you. Both Jesus and Rabbi Hillel thought this love-your-neighbor-as-yourself principle was a great place to start if you're looking for a guiding star.

Do the right thing means erring on the side of giving a bit more than what is required. Truth, honesty, and decency become your guide. *Do the right thing* gives that extra push that encourages you to take the lead—to take the first step—even when you don't have to. As I pointed out earlier, if you want something good to happen, someone has to be the first to say "I'm sorry" or "I love you" or "Let's try again." Why not decide to be that person?

I have found that a little extra kindness, humility, or generosity tends to set a positive cycle in motion. It tends to disarm the defensiveness and stinginess that so often take the wind out of the sails of healthy living. *Do the right thing* helps you call out the best in yourself and in other people, which can only tip the scales for the good. While it offers no guarantee of successfully influencing others, it does promise a high dividend yield in how you feel about yourself. You can bank on the fact that the guiding star of *do the right thing* will help you to both do better and feel better while doing it.

GUIDING STAR #3:
DO WHAT STRENGTHENS YOU AS A PERSON

What do you think about taking as your guiding star *do what strengthens you as a person?* Some people bristle at the idea, thinking it smacks of self-centeredness; making ourselves the reference point of our psychological world may sound a little suspect.

After all, it is not uncommon to look down on people who invest in their personal growth in therapy or other costly and time-consuming endeavors, thinking them navel gazers who are wasting their money on a self-indulgent luxury. It is easy to view those who seek self-improvement or pursue spiritual practices as a little bit kooky. Our culture has lost respect for those who take care to develop the interior life. Looking inward is thought to be a vice, not a virtue; a weakness, not a strength. In a culture that has become so Me-oriented, this judgment may sometimes be warranted.

There was a time when investment in self-development was considered a highly respectable endeavor, an aspiration, and even a guiding star. We looked up to those who conducted themselves with a sense of pride. By pride I do not mean arrogance or haughtiness or snootiness. I mean honor and self-respect and class. Children were taught to stand tall, tuck in their shirts, have good penmanship, and tell the truth. Adults prided themselves on using good manners, speaking respectfully to others, showing up on time (maybe even early), and doing their job well. We didn't cut so many corners. We built buildings and companies and ideas and self-respect that would last.

While it may sound a little old-fashioned in today's world, this kind of psychological framework goes a long way in developing a sense that your life means something. When you take pride of ownership in your life, you invest more seriously in how you go about living it. It doesn't mean that life is perfect. But taking pride in what you do and in who you are naturally generates a sense of being more solid, confident, and capable. You *feel* better because you are better.

If we translate these values into the psychological sphere, a picture comes into focus of what it means to be a stronger person. A psychologically strong person is grounded. He has legs underneath him to help him withstand the challenges of life. He has mental and emotional muscle, psychological meat on his bones. He is centered. He speaks his mind. He knows what he believes in. He follows his own conscience rather than the crowd. His roots run deep.

This reminds me of an image I have long carried of what I want to be like when I grow old. I picture myself in old age as a wide-hipped woman (talk about a countercultural image). While physical thinness may be a value in our American culture (especially for women), you can't be *emotionally* thin if you want to have a life that means something. Metaphorically speaking, a wise woman is going to have some hips. You'll think twice before trying to push her around!

In his letter to the folks at the church in ancient Galatia, St. Paul speaks about what it looks like to live a sturdy, meaningful, and spiritual life. He begins by pointing his readers to the guiding star of "Love your neighbor as yourself." But then he takes it a step further. He says that the spirit-filled life—a well-lived life— is characterized by some very substantial psychological capacities to which we all do well to aspire. He names them, one by one: love, joy, peace, patience, kindness, goodness, faithfulness, gentleness, and self-control (Galatians 5:22–23). If you're looking for a set of principles that have real substance—and you want them spelled out in detail—I urge you to take St. Paul's list as your guide.

Perhaps you can see the robustness of these psychological and spiritual capacities, and how they could lead to a life in which you would feel better, do better, and be better. When we conduct ourselves with love, joy, peace, and patience, we can feel good about the impact we have on others. When we are guided by kindness, goodness, faithfulness, gentleness, and self-control, we can take pride in the kind of person we are. Our roots grow deep; our hips grow wide. If, through each of our days and at the end of our days, we feel that we have invested ourselves in living an ethical, meaningful, and virtuous life, we are rich indeed.

GUIDING STAR #4: MAKE THE WORLD A BETTER PLACE

In his book *The Happiness Hypothesis*,[25] social psychologist Jonathan Haidt examines the extensive research on the factors that lead to happiness. He links a wide range of modern scientific studies with ancient philosophical wisdom, in search of the answer to the question "What makes us happy?" Ultimately, he agrees with Sigmund Freud that a balance of love and work is essential. However, he adds that those who find meaning and purpose in life—something even beyond happiness—are those who are able to find a connection to something greater than themselves. This is what I'm calling Guiding Star #4: *Make the world a better place*. You remember my instructor who said that Melanie Klein's model essentially comes down to one thing—love? Love is the name of the game. But the kind of love he was talking about—just like the kind of love Klein was talking about—is a love of a particular stripe. Love, in Klein's model, is defined as generosity that springs from gratitude. This is the kind of love that leads to a connection to something greater than ourselves. Guided by this type of love, we can't help but live in such a way that we make this world a better place.

Here's how it works. When we are able to make peace with our lives as they are, we are more and more able to see the good that is there. When we are able to set aside our grievances, forgive ourselves and our parents for failures and disappointments, and take the risk to engage in life just as it is, we shift our perspective. We see life more and more as the gift that it is. We feel grateful, fortunate, sometimes lucky, and even blessed. In my experience, this transformation can happen even for those who have been dealt a relatively weak hand. When the shift to gratitude happens in such meager circumstances, it's really something special.

When we are able to make peace with our lives as they are, we are more and more able to see the good that is there.

This inner transformation has a catalyzing effect on the human heart. It converts us to a new way of living. When we view ourselves as recipients of a precious gift, the impulse to generosity is turned on. We can't help but feel a desire to share from the goodness that we have been given.

Perhaps you've seen *Pay It Forward*, a film that poignantly takes up the theme of generosity. The main character is a seventh-grade student who is inspired to take seriously a class project assigned by his teacher. The assignment is to come up with an idea that would change the world for the better. This seventh-grader came up with an idea that would have made Melanie Klein beam with pride. He designed a program of generosity that springs from gratitude: Do a favor for someone—and don't be skimpy, it should be a real favor—and ask them to show their gratitude by "repaying" the favor *forward* to three other people.

The pay-it-forward project is based on the exponential formula of sharing with three friends, who share with three friends, who share with three friends, and so on, until you have a veritable explosion of generosity springing from gratitude. I love the powerful premise of the film and I love the fact that they don't portray it as being easy. Real-life difficulties emerge as the project is lived out. Homelessness, addiction, anger, grudges, resistance to change, and even death must be confronted. The film embraces the reality that gratitude and generosity aren't a panacea for the human condition. Nevertheless, it shows that, bit by bit, over time, people can change their attitudes toward themselves and other people in a way that contributes to positive change in the world.

As a guiding star, *make the world a better place* involves love, gratitude, and a sense of indebtedness that galvanizes the desire to give back and to give more. This more meaningful way of living involves sacrifice and the capacity to put someone else's needs ahead of your own. This mature kind of self-sacrifice should be distinguished from those that are much less healthy, like being a martyr or a doormat or a victim who cannot stand up for his needs. Mature self-sacrifice is rooted in a sense of having enough, even of having more than enough—that's the gratitude part. When we feel that our own cup runneth over due to the generosity of others, it is easy to give away some of the good that we have. In this vein, the psychological practice of self-sacrifice is a gift to the recipient as well as to the giver.

In one of my favorite little books called *Tales of a Magic Monastery*,[26] Theophane the Monk tells twelve stories about life—parables, really. In each story, a regular Joe or Jane takes a trip to the Magic Monastery, a pilgrimage to learn more about themselves, the world, and the Divine. I believe him when he says that all the stories are true, because they get to the heart of life's most important questions in a way that really gets your attention. The first story in the book is called "The Pearl of Great Price" and it's essentially a twist on a parable that Jesus told about the kingdom of heaven. In Jesus' version, a merchant set out to find the Pearl of Great Price and, when he found it, sold everything he had to buy it. The kingdom of heaven, Jesus suggested, is worth that much.

Theophane the Monk tells a different version of the story that really shakes things up. A pilgrim—a merchant, a regular Joe or Jane—goes to the Magic Monastery and asks one of the monks where he might find the Pearl of Great Price. To the pilgrim's great surprise, the monk simply reaches in his pocket and gives it to him. The pilgrim is shocked and in utter disbelief. Why would someone who possesses something of such great value just give it away? While the pilgrim reluctantly accepts the gift, he doesn't know what to do with it. Should he hide it? Should he share it? Should he spend it? As the story goes, the pilgrim is haunted for the rest of his life by the profound question—is it better to have the Pearl of Great price or to give it away?

If you take *make the world a better place* as your aspiration, you live out the answer to this question every day. If you're really paying attention, the answer is no great mystery; it is transparent in the details of the parable. Theophane the Monk shows us that if you have the Pearl of Great Price—I mean, really have it—then you'll understand that its true value is only found in giving it away.

The Pearl of Great Price is a symbol for this generosity-springing-from-gratitude kind of love. It is the final and most important lesson I hope to impart with this book. Its wisdom is wrapped in a paradox: Sacrificial love is the gift that keeps on giving.

I remember learning about this truth in elementary school music class when we sang the folk song "The Magic Penny."[27] The song's simple message is that love has a magical, mysterious property. Unlike most things in life, it is something that increases when you give it away. That's the paradox. When you share love, you do not lose; you gain. Love is something that if you give it away, you end up having more.

The idea of the magic penny is an important beginning to understanding the nature of love, but a bit more is needed if we want to see the whole picture. That's why I pair it with the other magic penny story—"The Pearl of Great Price"—because Theophane the Monk makes it clear that the kind of love that replenishes itself involves sacrifice. It costs you something. You must take the risk of giving away something valuable that you cherish, not knowing if it will ever come back to you. That's why we all gasp at the point in the story when the monk reaches in his pocket and just gives it away. That's the moment of sacrifice that is often so beyond us. That's the critical moment when we protest and the critical moment when we often get stuck. It turns out to be quite extraordinary to share something as ordinary as real love.

O. Henry captured the value of self-sacrificing love in his short story "The Gift of the Magi."[28] There are only two characters, a husband and wife, poor in means yet rich in love for each other. The setting is Christmas time, and they have no money for gifts for each other. The beauty of the story lies in their solution to this problem: The wife cuts and sells her hair to buy her husband a chain for his watch; the husband sells his watch to buy his wife a comb for her hair. It's just like that moment in "The Pearl of Great Price" when we gasp. This is real sacrifice that is extended out of real love. We can't help but weep and laugh at the same time as we bear witness to such a wonder.

I call Guiding Star #4 *make the world a better place*, but it could also be called *let love be your guide* or, as a pastor friend of mine calls it, *love is the name of the game.* If, by love, we mean self-sacrificing generosity that springs from gratitude, then we have taken something promising and reliable as our guide. If that is the spirit of our pursuits, then it doesn't really matter what we call it—what's most important is that we live it.

If you follow this guide, *make the world a better place* will really take you far. Your experiences along the way will not be all smiles and sunshine, but they will make a lasting imprint on your heart. They will deepen your sense of value and purpose, bringing a kind of fulfillment that is hard to find any other way.

There are some very practical ways in which one can live such a life. Raising children is one, as long as you really put your heart and soul and mind and sweat into it. Another involves doing work that contributes to the good by building something new or repairing what is broken. If you can, write a check to a worthy cause. That's a good place to start. But don't let it end there. Do something that makes and takes more than money. Take every opportunity to vote, say a prayer, volunteer, lend a hand. Stand up for what is right. Believe in something wholesome and good and true beyond reason, science, and chance. Pay special attention to the lost, the marginalized, the lonely, and the forgotten. Let your life mean something beyond your self-interest. Self-interest is a good thing, but once you have it, it is even better if you pay it forward—for its deeper value is found in giving it away.

IN CONCLUSION

CHANCES ARE, BY NOW, YOU understand why the greeting card I described at the beginning of this book made such an impression on me. When we stop and really think about it, we see that there are so many things to make in life besides money. I have tried to shine a light on some aspects of psychological life that I think hold the greatest value: love, peace, meaningful work, inner harmony, and developing a mind of one's own. I hope you will have discovered some valuable truths that were hiding in plain sight, perhaps eclipsed by our more routine strivings. Hopefully, you have gotten a better sense of what you're really looking for and how to go about finding it.

I am reminded of a story told of an old man who lost a coin one day at breakfast. When a friend came by later, he found him in the yard searching the ground.

"What are you doing?" the friend asked.

"Looking for the coin I dropped," the old man answered.

"Where did you lose it?"

"In the house."

"Then why are you out here?"

"Because," the old man replied, "the light is better out here."

Just like the old man, we are all seeking something on our psychological journey, but we often go about it all wrong. We take the easy way even though there is a better way. We stay outside where it is light rather than searching in the darkness inside—even though we know that's where our treasure lies.

When it comes to the error of our ways, we are in good company. Peter Pan, Jacob, the hare, Icarus, and the rest tried to bypass the hard work of facing life just as it is. They tried to cut corners, take shortcuts, and make up their own rules. But their tactics wound up making things worse, as such tactics always do. That is why their stories are cautionary tales. That's why we try to learn from them rather than keep repeating them, over and over again.

When we develop a clear understanding of how our minds operate, we are able to make the kind of change that impacts us at the core, the kind of change that lasts.

I have tried to show you an alternative way of approaching life, a way that is much more likely to work. With the wisdom of psychoanalysis as our guide, we are able to go deeper in addressing the challenges of our lives. By understanding the unconscious and internal factors that influence us, we are able to treat our struggles at their root. This allows us to grow ourselves from the ground up—and from the inside out.

When we develop a clear understanding of how our minds operate, we are able to make the kind of change that impacts us at the core, the kind of change that lasts. Then life becomes more than sprucing up the exterior or rearranging the seats on the *Titanic*. Then we discover that there are ways to change our course the necessary few degrees to keep us moving in the right direction. Making that small shift is all we can do in this life—and all that needs to be done.

This deeper, more effective approach to our psychological journey is not an easy one, but it is extremely worthwhile. As I've said before, I can't really prove its worth to you. I can't take it to the bank or the research lab to have its value assessed. As the saying goes, not everything that counts can be counted, and not everything that can be counted counts. So there's got to be some faith and trust involved in choosing this more meaningful way. At the very least, I hope to have inspired you to consider giving it a try. Sometimes you just have to accept the pearl that has been given to you, try to do some good with it, and find out where it takes you. Whatever path you choose, it's up to you.

It's always up to you.

ENDNOTES

1. David Dark, *The Sacredness of Questioning Everything* (Grand Rapids, MI: Zondervan, 2009).

2. Randall Sorenson, *Minding Spirituality* (London: Routledge, 2004).

3. For further reading see Melanie Klein, *Love, Guilt and Reparation: And Other Works 1921–1945* (London: Hogarth Press, 1975); Melanie Klein, *Envy and Gratitude: And Other Works 1946–1963* (London: Hogarth Press, 1975).

4. Alessandra Piontelli, *Backwards in Time: A Study in Infant Observation by the Method of Esther Bick* (London: The Clunie Press, 1986).

5. Henry Cloud, *Changes That Heal* (Grand Rapids, MI: Zondervan, 1990).

6. Sigmund Freud, *On Beginning the Treatment*, standard ed., vol. 12 (London: Hogarth Press, 1913), 129.

7. Bhante Gunaratana, *Mindfulness in Plain English* (Somerville, MA: Wisdom Publications, 2002), 91.

8. Ibid., 35.

9. M. Scott Peck, *The Road Less Traveled*, 25th Anniversary Ed. (New York: Touchstone, 2003), 15.

10. See Joanne Greenberg, *I Never Promised You a Rose Garden* (New York: St. Martin's Press, 1964).

11. Margery Williams, *The Velveteen Rabbit: Or How Toys Become Real* (London: Heinemann, 1922).

12. Bronnie Ware, *The Top Five Regrets of the Dying* (Carlsbad, CA: Hay House, 2012).

13. Reinhold Niebuhr, *The Essential Reinhold Niebuhr: Selected Essays and Addresses*, ed. Robert McAfee Brown (New Haven, CT: Yale University Press, 1987), 251.

14. Ruth Harms Calkin, *Tell Me Again, Lord, I Forget* (Carol Stream, IL: Tyndale House, 1986).

15. Antonio Damasio, *The Feeling of What Happens: Body and Emotion in the Making of Consciousness* (Orlando, FL: Mariner Books, 2000).

16. Marsha Linehan, *Skills Training Manual for Treating Borderline Personality Disorder* (New York: Guilford Press, 1993).

17. Donald Meltzer, *Sexual States of Mind* (London: Karnac, 1973), 78.

18. Helen Keller, *The Story of My Life* (New York: Grosset & Dunlap, 1902, 1903, 1905), 38–39.

19. Ibid.

20. Melanie Klein, "Love, Guilt and Reparation" (1937), in *Love, Guilt and Reparation: And Other Works 1921–1945* (London: Hogarth Press, 1975), 306–343.

21. Michael Chester, *Divine Pathos and Human Being: The Theology of Abraham Joshua Heschel* (London: Vallentine Mitchell, 2005).

22. Rainer Maria Rilke, *Letters to a Young Poet*, trans. M. D. Herter Norton (New York: W. W. Norton & Company, 1934, 1954, renewed © 1962, 1982 by M. D. Herter Norton).

23. Kahlil Gibran, *The Prophet*, (London: Wordsworth Editions, 1997).

24. Henri Nouwen, *Bread for the Journey: A Daybook of Wisdom and Faith* (New York: HarperCollins, 1997).

25. Jonathan Haidt, *The Happiness Hypothesis: Finding Modern Truth in Ancient Wisdom* (New York: Basic Books, 2006).

26. Theophane the Monk, *Tales of a Magic Monastery* (New York: Crossroad Publishing, 1995).

27. Malvina Reynold, "The Magic Penny" (copyright by Northern Music Corporation, 1955).

28. O. Henry, *The Four Million* (New York: Doubleday, Page, and Company, 1906).